FORGOTTEN RAILWAYS:

East Anglia

THE FORGOTTEN RAILWAYS SERIES

Edited by J. Allan Patmore

North East England by K. Hoole

The East Midlands by P. Howard Anderson

Chilterns & Cotswolds by R. Davies and M. D. Grant

North and Mid Wales by Rex Christiansen

Scotland by John Thomas

South East England by H. P. White

FORGOTTEN RAILWAYS:

East Anglia

R. S. JOBY

DAVID & CHARLES
NEWTON ABBOT   LONDON
NORTH POMFRET (VT)

ISBN o 7153 7312 9

Library of Congress Catalog Card Number 76–48824

© R. S. Joby 1977

First published 1977
Second impression 1977
Third impression 1979

Printed in Great Britain by
Redwood Burn Limited, Trowbridge & Esher
for David & Charles (Publishers) Limited
Brunel House   Newton Abbot   Devon

Published in the United States of America
by David & Charles Inc
North Pomfret   Vermont 05053   USA

Contents

Introduction

A small 2–4–0 tender engine, with tall stovepipe chimney, towing a couple of elderly corridor coaches, drifts to a stop at a short low platform. Platform is perhaps an exaggeration for there is little more than a levelled heap of ashes and clinker fronted by three or four rows of sleepers to form the edge. At the back of the platform an old coach body serves as a waiting room, with a solitary oil lamp fixed to the outside for night-time illumination. Surrounding the station are fields and hedges, a cottage or two near a level-crossing carrying a road across the railway and little else.

A passenger gets out, a couple get on; sometimes there is nobody. The Westinghouse pump on the engine lazily pants away to restore pressure to the braking system, for this is the land of air brakes, at least on locomotives; the guard raises a hand, a short whistle shrieks from the engine in response and the train starts on its way again. The guard wanders down the corridor, money bag slung across his shoulder and ticket rack in hand, to take the fares of newcomers to the train, for conductor guards are not new to this part of the world.

The coaches have seen better days and when built before World War I graced such trains as the Norfolk Coast Express or perhaps the Hook Continental. Now their age shows, the wooden panels creak as the train ambles through the rolling countryside, and the seats are faded and worn. One is an open saloon coach with a guard's compartment, and folding steps from the one passenger door give access to low platforms; the other has a side corridor with first and third class compartments. One of the latter at the end has two curiously hidden seats tucked away behind the end corridor partition where seemingly the designer forgot until the last minute that the corridor to the end gangway and the end compartment were competing for the same space! A few trains even in 1950 still had six-wheel coaches, and gas-lit bogie coaches with clerestory roofs lasted a few years longer.

Such a station scene could be observed at many places in East Anglia, right up to the late 1950s, for it was typical of the branch and cross country lines which made up so much railway mileage in Essex, Suffolk and Norfolk. Not all stations were so primitive; many country stations were smart substantially-built brick structures, some of which on closed lines survive now in other uses.

Today the railways they served are but memories, and while for many areas the coming and going of the railway has turned full circle, a century or so of railways has changed the social and economic life of a part of the country that still contrasts vividly between an expanding London commuter belt stretching well into Essex and dying isolated rural hamlets in Norfolk.

East Anglia had most of its railway mileage built in the latter half of the nineteenth century. The main line pattern was clear by 1849, with the London–Cambridge–Norwich–Yarmouth route forming the backbone of the system; that to Norwich via Ipswich had only just been completed by the Eastern Union Railway, only later becoming the preferred route to Norwich from London. A small system radiated from King's Lynn, with a line joining the Norwich–Cambridge–London route at Ely. This left large areas of farmland and many small towns distant from railways and thus at an economic disadvantage.

The dominant Eastern Counties Railway took over the running of other major railways in East Anglia. The East Anglian, Norfolk, Northern & Eastern and the Eastern Union were operated as a single system with the Eastern Counties Railway, which gained a bad reputation for poor, slow services and for exhibiting an attitude to its customers that bore the worst signs of monopoly practice. As a poor railway it had no money for expansion and up to its demise in 1862 built very few new lines. Thus any districts which wanted the benefits of railway access had to promote their own lines and either run them themselves, or come to agreements favourable to the Eastern Counties, allowing the main line company to run the lines at between fifty and seventy per cent of gross receipts.

East Anglia really awoke to the possibilities of supplying industrial areas with more of its products on a large scale in the second half of the nineteenth century. Although there were no coal mines, and few other minerals of value, farm produce, fish, and specialised manufactures which required little fuel in their production were all available for marketing elsewhere. The problem was to transport these items cheaply from their points of production to London, Manchester and elsewhere, so that they were still competitive with similar produce. Average charges for horse-and-cart transport in the mid-nineteenth century were about 4p (9½d) per ton per mile. Thus if the nearest station were twenty miles away, it cost 80p per ton just to carry goods to and fro. If a railway were built, the cost of carriage was brought down to between ½p and 2p per ton per mile, which meant either more profit to the producer or a greatly reduced, and thus more attractive, selling price. Even if the railway as such was not likely to make a profit when built, it was still worthwhile having it in order to be competitive with areas that had railways.

Yarmouth and Lowestoft had been popular resorts even before the railways came, and from the time that lines arrived at these towns in the 1840s the numbers of visitors and the scale of accommodation and entertainment available for them rose by leaps and bounds. Other places along the East Anglian coast had railways built to them, starting with the Lynn & Hunstanton Railway in 1862. This was an instant success and later paid a 10 per cent dividend, a rarity for a nineteenth-century English line, and consequently there were many imitators. The attraction of seaside railways increased when Bank Holidays were introduced from 1871. Lines to Cromer, Clacton, Southwold, Aldebùrgh, Felixstowe, a second line to Southend, and other lines to Cromer, Yarmouth, Lowestoft were built.

The fishing industry started to supply large quantities of fresh fish as well as the smoked, dried and salted varieties of earlier periods. Railways took fish quickly to inland markets, and direct delivery of fish by boat to Billingsgate declined. Dockside tramways ensured that the fish was sent away as rapidly as possible. Attempts were made to create major new fishing ports at Southwold, Blakeney and Harwich on the basis of expanding existing small old ones, but all these failed.

Late nineteenth-century East Anglia was alive to economic developments, and farming changed to meet new demands. As cheap overseas wheat flooded in, the farmers in progressive areas started to grow fruit, vegetables and, nearer London, to raise dairy cows. Tramways and light railways were built to transport these crops cheaply and efficiently. The superb quality of East Anglian malting barley was not approached by imports, so brewers expanded their East Anglian maltings alongside railways and paid good prices at a time when other grains were cheap. The malt was then sent to London, Burton-on-Trent, Newcastle and other brewing centres by rail.

The advent of the Great Eastern Railway in 1862 was important because the successor to the Eastern Counties Railway was expansion-minded and intent on helping the local economy. It was a far more benevolent monopoly which built some new lines of its own and encouraged others with management expertise and capital. Services were improved and speeded up, traffic sought and encouraged wherever it could be found, and new traffic brought through East Anglia by the construction of a joint line with the Great Northern Railway to bring coal from the Nottinghamshire coalfield to London.

Although its profits never compared with those of the London & North Western or the North Eastern Railway, the Great Eastern prospered quietly in the late nineteenth century and drew envious eyes towards capturing some of that traffic. The Midland & Great Northern Joint Railway is probably the best known interloper in East Anglia. This railway took traffic westwards, at right-angles to the Great Eastern's flow of traffic; it built up a huge holiday traffic to Norfolk and north Suffolk resorts, but was less successful in wresting other traffic from the Great Eastern. It did however inject competition into East Anglia and lowered rates right across Norfolk, to the benefit of farmers.

Railways continued to be built right up to the eve of World War I. Joint lines and light railways were the fashion in the first decade of the twentieth century. The roads were usually very poor and few motorbuses ran before 1919, most of them being owned and operated by the Great Eastern Railway. Horse-and-cart was still the most common way of transporting goods to and from stations until the 1930s, slow and expensive though it was.

The coming of mass-produced motor vehicles, tarred all-weather roads and widespread garages in the 1920s altered the picture completely for the railways. Many lines lost their passenger services between 1927 and 1931; one line closed completely in 1929. Thereafter the railways in East Anglia were fighting a rearguard action against road transport except during the war years 1939–45. Local passengers deserted to the buses, goods traffic declined, and holidaymakers started to come in their own cars.

These traffic losses increased after 1945, and from 1951 branch lines started to close in increasing numbers. Usually passenger services ceased first then goods sections were closed until in 1959 much of the M&GN system was closed completely.

The Beeching Report sealed the fate of many branches in the 1960s. The closing of individual station goods yards left many branches with no function other than carrying a handful of passengers, and once the bus companies were persuaded to alter their services to cater for these passengers the whole line closed. Excursion traffic to the seaside declined, summer holiday passengers changed to cars and coaches to the extent that ninety-seven per cent of Cromer's holiday-makers and day-trippers arrived by road in 1966.

Nowadays a stark skeleton of the former network survives. Several of the remaining lines are reprieved on a year-to-year basis and only the original main lines make a clear profit. As one passes isolated signal boxes along the main lines, one sees a cutting or embankment curving away into the distance, a reminder of a once-busy junction with a station staff of half-a-dozen or more, where the branch line train once waited in the siding to take connecting passengers to quiet market towns. Each line had distinctive features of its own, its own endearing idiosyncrasies. The object of this book is to revive memories of these lines and provide a guide to the plentiful remains which can be seen by walker, cyclist and car driver. Isolated signal boxes, a dozen miles from the nearest used track, growing tomatoes now, earthworks, station buildings and other memorabilia abound throughout East Anglia to stir nostalgic memories in those old enough to have travelled on the forgotten lines, or to give a solid basis for the imaginations of those of lesser years. Many regret the passing of these delightful lines which helped the East Anglian economy through a very difficult period.

CHAPTER 1

Mid-Essex & North-East Hertfordshire

What is now the commuter fringe of North-East London contained several branches of a very individual character. First to be built was the line from Braintree to Maldon, at a right-angle to the Eastern Counties main line. Originally intended to be a through line, it was built as a pair of branches from Witham and opened in 1848. The Witham–Braintree line survives as a commuter branch but the line down to the coastal part of Maldon was torn up after the line finally closed to goods traffic on 18 April 1966.

The ancient port of Maldon was the junction for a link to Woodham Ferrers, part of the New Essex Lines of the GER. Having been denied access to Southend, the GER determined to build its own branch from the main line at Shenfield together with a branch to Southminster along the Crouch valley and link this with the Maldon branch by a line from Woodham Ferrers. Triangular junctions were built at Witham, Maldon and Wickford to permit through running of excursion trains from the Colchester line. Seaside excursions were hugely popular elsewhere and the greater the number of destinations possible the greater the growth of traffic that could be catered for—or so ran official thinking. This was not to be; the traffic did not prosper, nor did the intermediate traffic despite efforts to encourage it by building halts en route. Despite proximity to London, commuters did not settle in this bleak part of Essex, and with a settlement bearing a name like Cold Norton halfway who could blame them?

13

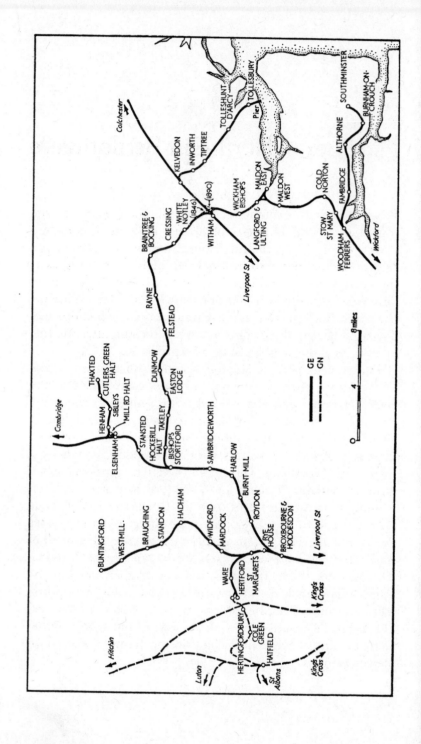

The other branch down to the muddy Essex creeks was the Kelvedon, Tiptree & Tollesbury Pier Light Railway, authorised by the Board of Trade on 8 January 1901. There was only one bridge to build and earthworks were light, but it still took two hundred men two years to build the line as far as Tollesbury. The final 1½ miles to the lengthy wooden pier at Tollesbury was not ready until 15 May 1907. Weekend and holiday leisure pursuits were a growth industry in Edwardian England and it was hoped that yachting, weekend bungalows and even packet boats to the continent would 'develop at Tollesbury Pier.

Such hopes as these were unrealistic for a line, so lightly-built, sharply-curved and with a ruling gradient of 1 in 50, not to mention an axle weight restriction of 14 tons and a 16mph speed limit reduced to 10mph within 200yd of level-crossings. Harwich was the established packet station of the parent GER and would be unlikely to aid a rival at Tollesbury. The muddy foreshore at Tollesbury was unattractive as a resort in comparison with sandy Clacton, and there were many better-placed rivals for yachting.

The Kelvedon & Tollesbury Light Railway settled down to a humble existence hauling coal and agricultural supplies into its district and taking out farm produce and the famous Tiptree jams; passenger services were particularly sketchy. An initial service of four trains each way per day was reduced to three after only four months, but had returned to four each way by 1923 with additional trains on Wednesdays and Fridays for local markets. Tollesbury Pier was served by trains 'which would run to or from Pier Station when necessary.' Most trains were mixed, with shunting taking up time at intermediate stations. Average speeds for the full journey were between 8mph and 14mph, no match for the bus competition of the 1920s and later. A shunter travelled on mixed trains and opened the points with the Annett's key at stations and goods sidings.

For the railway enthusiast, if not for the regular passenger, the chief attraction of a journey to Tollesbury was the unique train which simmered in the low-level station at Kelvedon, awaiting the connection from Liverpool Street. From 1905 the locomotive was a J67 0–6–0 tank, in the early years converted to a 2–4–0 tank by the simple expedient of removing the forward coupling rods, hopefully to counter the high level of wear-and-tear engendered by the sharp curvature of the line. This was always evident from the metallic screeching which accompanied the slow, wallowing movement of the train. With only one engine in steam and a regular crew the locomotive was usually one of the cleanest on the line.

Carriages were also unique. Until 1928 the stock was six-wheeled, one class only (third) with centre gangway for the conductor-guard. Retractable steps permitted entry to carriages from the rail-level platforms. The closure of the Wisbech & Upwell to passengers released the tramway-type coaches for which the Kelvedon & Tollesbury is best remembered. The older four-wheeled stock was little used but the bogie coaches lasted until the end of passenger services in 1951. The passengers sat facing each other inside the gas-lit carriages as they lurched and squealed around the curves. At every level-crossing or station there was a thump from behind as the goods wagons rolled forward after the carriages had been braked. On starting again there was a snatching feeling as the train picked up speed.

The conductor-guard issued bus-type tickets after finding out the destinations of the passengers. He would first go the length of the train, crossing the heaving drop-plates between the carriages with considerable agility, and then punch the tickets in his van before issuing them to the passengers. With only a dozen or so passengers, and few joining or leaving at intermediate stations except Tiptree this, combined with gate closing, parcels work and normal guards' duties, gave him a varied and interesting working life. For the

Plates 1 and 2. The M&GN flavour. *Above:* Beyer Peacock 4–4–0 No 29 on Cromer train, at Sheringham, 1933. *Below:* Class 4MT 2–6–0 No 43150 approaching Melton Constable. *(Dr I. C. Allen)*

Plates 3 and 4. Above: Great Yarmouth Beach station in August 1931, today a coach station and car park. *Below:* Breydon Viaduct carrying the Midland & Great Northern spur over Breydon Water from Yarmouth Beach towards Lowestoft. *(L&GRP)*

passenger, a great illicit pleasure was to ride on the open balconies of the carriages, rare indeed in Britain.

Kelvedon Low Level, Tiptree and Tollesbury all had typical light railway wooden stations with low platforms. Elsewhere old carriages, and at Feering Halt an old bus body, sufficed. Only Tiptree and Tollesbury were staffed.

Yet before the advent of improved roads and reliable buses the value of such a quaint byway must not be understated. The fruit-growers of the Tiptree district had reason to be thankful for a local siding, saving them a long 2mph return trek to Kelvedon or Witham by horse-and-cart. Market days were much easier with the railway and more distant markets could be reached, to the benefit of the local farmer and orchardist.

This part of Essex is best seen in blossom time, when it is difficult to believe that a railway of such unique eccentricity could exist, yet be within an hour's journey of London. A mile or so away from Kelvedon and one is a world away from the mad rush of the A12 or the Inter-City trains which speed through the main station at Kelvedon.

Bishop's Stortford, Dunmow & Braintree Railway

Linking the Essex coast lines with the Cambridge main line was the Bishop's Stortford, Dunmow & Braintree Railway, a cross-country line which got into difficulties long before it was opened and which had to be taken-over by the Great Eastern Railway in order to finance its completion and opening in 1869. This gave the GER four effective east–west lines between its two major north–south lines, but the line from Bishop's Stortford was rarely used as such except for excursions from Bishop's Stortford to the Essex coast, and spent most of its life serving the farmers with passenger services to Braintree only and pick-up goods services for the very productive arable countryside through which it passed. The Traffic Department was, however, always on the lookout for further traffic and opened Hockerill Halt in 1910 to serve the nearby golf course. In the days before motor cars this was an admirable route to and from the 19th hole in the club house.

The liveliest period for goods services was always the sugar beet season. Felstead sugar factory was opened in the 1920s as part of the government's plans to diversify agriculture and make Great Britain less dependent on overseas producers in the aftermath of war. From September to January a procession of goods trains laden with coal, lime and, as the season progressed, sugar beet rolled towards the factory from all over north Essex and nearby Hertfordshire. Ex-GER 0–6–0s slowly thumped and clanked their heavy loads along. Station yards were often filled with two-wheel tipping horse-carts when wagons were awaited. The British Sugar Corporation was and still is very rail-minded and did much in the inter-war period to prevent the fortunes of such branch lines falling further than they did.

The Elsenham & Thaxted Light Railway

A few miles north of Bishop's Stortford a light railway similar in some respects to the Kelvedon & Tollesbury was built between Elsenham station on the main Cambridge line and a field across the valley from the historic town of Thaxted. The locally-promoted Elsenham & Thaxted Light Railway was intended to relieve agricultural distress and to be extended to Great Bardfield, over ten miles from Elsenham. In the event, despite the GER paying half the capital cost and a large grant of £33,000 from the Treasury, little local capital was raised and there was a five-year interlude between the granting of the Light Railway order in 1906 and the start of construction in 1911.

The line eventually stopped a mile short of Thaxted church and was opened on 1 April 1913. Typically of light railways of the period the Elsenham & Thaxted was built with few earthworks, steep gradients, only one bridge, and ungated level-crossings with cattle guards wherever possible.

The scene at Elsenham was in marked contrast to the main line. On the sharply-curved branch platform a small GER o–6–o tank or occasionally a J15 tender o–6–o stood at the head of a short rake of very elderly GER six-wheeled coaches. There was the connection with the main line and a small goods yard. The passengers were usually few in number. A few trucks generally followed the passenger coaches. The conductor-guard issued thin white paper tickets straight to the passengers like a bus conductor; there were no through bookings. A sharp blast of the whistle and the locomotive chuntered away, puffing harder and harder as it breasted the long 1 in 50 gradient out of Elsenham onto the high open plateaux of Essex. The train slowed down to 10mph for the ungated crossings at Mill Road and Henham, picking-up or setting-down at the halts if necessary. At Sibleys (for Chickney & Broxted), to give the full title, the train usually stopped to shunt by towrope. There was a goods loop at this station, so that by attaching the towrope to wagons in the adjacent loop the train engine could manoeuvre them from the other track. This diversion took up to ten minutes in the busy season. The penultimate halt at Cutler's Green was distinguished by only having footpath access to the low cinder platform with an old coach body as a waiting room. Thaxted was reached in about half-an-hour from Elsenham, a small single-platform station with a run-round loop and a corrugated iron locomotive shed. Passengers alighting at Thaxted then walked across the Chelmer Valley to town; this saved the railway the building cost but crippled its defensive ability when buses lifted passengers from the centre of the town more swiftly and conveniently to nearby shopping centres. A pleasant line in the midst of High Essex, it was an early victim of closure as it was slow and poorly connected for passengers and only offered two sidings for goods, so that goods services ceased less than a year after passenger trains stopped running in 1952.

The Ware, Hadham & Buntingford Railway

Buntingford was one of the many thriving market towns in East Anglia that was missed by chance or design by the main lines, and which decided to build its own connection to the main line railway. The Ware, Hadham & Buntingford Railway, despite its name, never went to Ware but made its junction with the Great Eastern Hertford branch further south at St Margaret's, to avoid offending a landowner. This line had more than its share of troubles. Its contractor, W. S. Simpson of Ely, used low-grade timber on the bridge at Westmill, which was completely rotten by 1868. Earlier the bridge at Braughing had failed even before opening. Yet the same contractor was employed by the East Norfolk Railway after this job. To these troubles was added the high cost of compensating other landowners along the route, and but for aid by the ECR and later the GER its fate would have been similiar to the Mistley, Thorpe & Walton Railway of the same period. The line prospered despite its birth pangs, traffic increased and most of the line and its stations were rebuilt before the turn of the century.

The growth of the London residential fringe overtook North-East Hertfordshire by the 1920s when through trains to Liverpool Street were run. Leafy abodes little more than an hour away from the City were increasingly sought by the discerning, and the charming timbered villages and hilly countryside around Buntingford offered everything that Metroland had, without the crowds. Walkers were encouraged to use the branch with cheap Sunday tickets. Goods traffic was not so healthy, however, and the service of three goods trains a day, operated prior to World War I, fell to only one except at busy times.

The typical inter-war business train on the Buntingford

branch was worked by a smartly-polished 'Gobbler' 2–4–2T hauling a rake of teak coaches with large gold-leaf '1' and '3' figures denoting class on the doors. The black homburg-hatted clerks quickly boarded, untroubled by females, and maintained something of a club atmosphere in the trains right up to World War II. Later in the morning some of the wives followed in a later train for a day's shopping in the West End. These were the peak years which continued until the mid 1950s, when car ownership allowed commuters to try Bishop's Stortford and the Great Northern stations from which much faster trains ran, King's Cross being far more convenient for the West End offices. Few middle-of-the-day trains had more than a handful of passengers and by November 1960 these were eliminated. The business trains direct to London ceased and the choice of motoring to a main line station became more attractive than a dmu with a change to electric train at St Margaret's. The route of this line is best seen today in the autumn. The deep beech-clothed valleys of the Chilterns through which the little branch travelled are then at their best: the villages look perfect in the calm air of an autumn evening and summer's crowds are far away.

Welwyn to Hertford

Nearby was the Welwyn–Hertford branch of the GNR. Originally part of a line from Luton to Hertford which had hopes of being an important cross-country link, this branch had direct competition from the GER into Hertford; the GNR then built its own direct line through Hertford, leaving the branch almost without purpose. The GNR, like its successor the LNER, was never a railway to give up a line easily and the Welwyn to Hertford line saw a succession of experiments in running a branch line cheaply. Early in the century a rail-motor, a diminutive locomotive attached to a bogie coach was tried, with indifferent results. The chief problem of this arrangement was that of housing the rail-motor for servicing when off-duty—in a conventional locomotive depot like Hatfield the carriage became saturated with smoke and the upholstery soon became dirty and smelly. It was very difficult to detach either part of the rail-motor if there were a mechanical failure, while there was no possibility of adding many carriages or combining with the daily goods train when traffic fluctuated a lot.

A second effort was made in the 1930s with the 300hp Sentinel-Cammell steam railcars named after stage-coaches. The rapid start-up of the water-tube boilers, steam-heating and electric lighting made them popular with passengers and a crew of two made them cheaper to operate than conventional branch line stock, yet a capacity of only forty-eight passengers did not cater for peaks, and mixed trains apart from a van or two were not possible. The branch benefitted a little from the expansion of Welwyn Garden City but less than from conventional suburban expansion as Welwyn was designed to be self-contained. The branch was closed before the New Towns of Hatfield, Welwyn and Stevenage rejuvenated the area's rail traffic in the late 1950s; it is a monument to the perils of Victorian over-building without traffic research.

CHAPTER 2

North-East Norfolk

Of all the districts of East Anglia, North-East Norfolk was alone in being without railway communication until as late as 1874. Plans for a North of Norfolk Railway in 1845 came in for adverse criticism 'as to the probable dearth of traffic', and were dropped. Subsequent proposals by the Norfolk Railway and the Ipswich, Bury & Norwich Company to enter this area were mutually destructive, and were dropped in the aftermath of the Railway Mania. Not until 1865 were the first rails laid north of Norwich in this district, and financial difficulties prevented the opening of the first section until October 1874. Yet a mere thirteen years later the system was nearly complete in its final form, apart from the North Walsham–Mundesley–Cromer lines. Cromer, North Walsham, Reepham, Fakenham and Worstead (Honing for Worstead) each had two stations, Yarmouth and Norwich had had a third added. Such was the extent of competition which suddenly flooded this remote and rural area with an abundance of railway facilities.

The East Norfolk Railway, which built the Whitlingham Junction–Cromer and Wroxham–Reepham lines, still exists almost in its entirety and thus is not the concern of this chapter. The lines which have closed are those which became the Midland & Great Northern Joint Railway in 1893. Only the Cromer–Weybourne, and Themelthorpe–Lenwade sections remain open. Of the short-lived Norfolk & Suffolk Joint, only Roughton Road Junction to Cromer survives. The first total closure came as late as 15 September 1952,

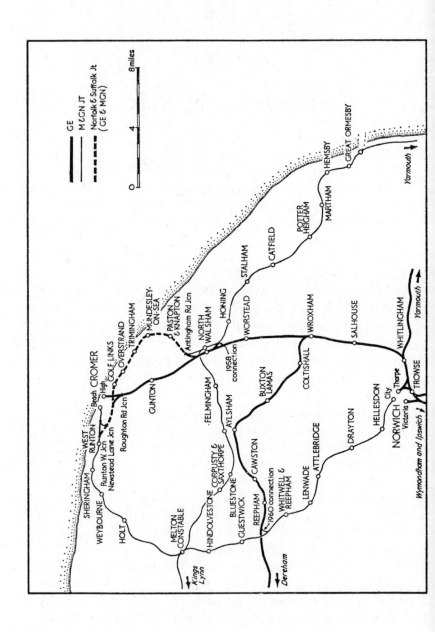

from Foulsham to Reepham, followed by Mundesley to Cromer the following April. The biggest blow was the closure of much of the M&GN on 28 February 1959, and by 1964 the present stage had been reached apart from Lenwade to Norwich City, goods only, which closed down only when its coal traffic was transferred to a new depot. At the time of writing, the rails were still in place as far as Attlebridge.

While the East Norfolk Railway was slowly being built towards Cromer, an independent light railway from Great Yarmouth to Stalham was authorised by Act of Parliament in 1876. Two years later, and long before reaching Stalham, its extension to North Walsham had been authorised by a further Act, while in the following year additional Acts authorised a long extension to connect with the Lynn & Fakenham Railway at Pudding Norton. The same Act authorised a change of name to the Yarmouth & North Norfolk Railway, and the building of dock tramways in Yarmouth. Thus was born the connection with the Midland Railway and the Great Northern Railway via King's Lynn and Peterborough, which developed into the Eastern & Midlands Railway on 1 January 1883 and, after the building of the Cromer branch and the direct link to the Midland Railway, into the Midland & Great Northern Joint Railway on 1 July 1893.

There was much support in North Norfolk for a railway independent of the monopolistic Great Eastern, which by 1881 had absorbed the slow-growing and inconveniently-timetabled East Norfolk Railway. Local landowners, especially Lord Hastings of Melton Hall, took an active role in promoting the Eastern & Midlands and its predecessors. In so doing they would obtain better communications for themselves and for their produce with the world outside Norfolk and would also benefit the locality as a whole by shortening distances between farms and railway, allow coal to be brought in more cheaply and allow new industries to develop.

27

Both the Lynn & Fakenham and the Yarmouth & North Norfolk Railways were 'contractors' lines. In both cases Messrs Wilkinson & Jarvis of London built a line as a speculation, raising money by bonds, debentures and mortgages, hoping to sell it to a larger railway company on or preferably prior to completion. An employee of the contractors, William Marriott, became engineer to the new company in 1883, two years after finishing his apprenticeship. He added the locomotive superintendency to his duties the following year and became traffic manager as well in 1919, finally retiring in 1924. Having helped build the line together with its traffic and repair centre, Melton Constable, he lived there for some years during the early development of the community.

Almost from the beginning, then, the Eastern & Midlands Railway was strongly influenced by Marriott. He scoured Norfolk for bricks, established a railway colony in the wilds of North Norfolk, designed and improvised, keeping the railway going in good times and bad for over forty years. Money was always short, the amount of capital and loan stock to be serviced over £2¼ million, yet a very creditable service was built up in territory which had little industry and was suffering from agricultural depression.

Melton Constable developed rapidly, both as a junction and works village. From a parish population of 118 in 1881, and with no settlement on the present site, it grew to a population of 1,157 in 1911, but this has subsequently fallen to about 650 today. All M&GN traffic from and to the west had to pass through Melton Constable, and from 1887 trains from King's Lynn gave connections to Cromer, Norwich and Yarmouth, while by 1903 Lowestoft and Mundesley were also accessible. A long island platform with refreshment room and all the usual offices formed the hub of the system. Here trains divided or were made up when proceeding west, freight trains were shunted and assembled, locomotives serviced in the running shed, and repairs to equipment carried out. Labour was difficult to obtain and retain in such an isolated spot in the early days.

Houses were built by a contractor on an undertaking by the company to pay the rents. The early houses in Melton Street and Astley Terrace, built for £150 each, are of poor quality, but have recently been refurbished. Later houses in Colville Road and Briston Road are of better quality, built after the setting-up of the Joint committee, when more money was available. Melton Street in particular looked like a transplant from an East Midlands industrial town. The street itself is narrow, the front gardens tiny and the larger houses, valued originally at £250 each, at the ends of each terrace add an oppressiveness to the view. The larger houses were for the doctor and supervisory staff. Facing the bowling green is a short terrace of six bow-windowed houses of better construction. Colman's grocery, built and opened in 1894, has remained in the same family ever since. Close proximity to the works had great advantages, and the factory hooter dominated life in Melton Constable even for the few non-railway inhabitants.

The works buildings, of brick and iron construction, are of good quality; most are still extant, forming the basis of a trading estate. Other facilities, distinctly rare in North Norfolk at the period, included gasworks, water tower and sewage works, all of which, apart from the gas-holders, can still be seen. A feature of the station was Lord Hastings' private waiting-room on the south side of the platform, complete with private drive and platform. The building has recently been demolished, and drive and platform have been covered by a road development. Lord Hastings financed an hotel bearing his name, sold land north of the railway houses for private development and, with the company, built an elementary school, which is now the primary school. The Railway Institute of 1896, the recreation ground and bowling greens catered for leisure and part-time education needs, while the Mission Hall just inside the neighbouring parish of Briston kept some workers away from the demon drink. A close and distinctive community came into being in the late nineteenth century, in appearance and type quite different from any other in North Norfolk. Apart from the rail tracks, most of it remains a perfect miniature fossil railway town, with little subsequently destroyed as in so many others.

The completed railway desperately required traffic. The locomotive stock was more suited to the rural railway origins of the line, apart from new Class A Beyer Peacock 4–4–0 express locomotives which came into service from 1882 when an initial four were delivered. Much of the track, laid for rural lines, was light and poorly ballasted. Most of the line was single-track, and consequently early express speeds averaged little over 32mph. Subsequent track improvements, track doubling between Raynham Park and Corpusty, and the installation of tablet catchers on the locomotives raised averaged speeds to nearly 44mph between Melton Constable and King's Lynn by 1903, by which date the full effects of the 1893 Joint changes and improvements were evident. Through passenger expresses were being run by 1906 from London in the south to Liverpool in the north, and connections were offered to most parts of the country, many faster than by the Great Eastern.

Holidays for the masses rather than the selected few became common in the 1880s, and thanks largely to the M&GN, North Norfolk got a share of this trade. A line of large redbrick hotels arose on the cliff tops between Weybourne and Mundesley, while established Yarmouth's facilities were also expanded. The Midland Railway, eager to feed traffic on to its Joint protégé, published a booklet in 1894 of available farmhouse accommodation on the North Norfolk Coast. Families often hired cottages for the summer, and fathers were encouraged to visit at weekends. Wherries on the Broads were being converted for leisure use by the 1890s, and added to the pleasure traffic. The main problem with this traffic was that it was summers only, and largely concentrated on Saturdays, when returning holidaymakers went home from the coast in the morning, and the new arrivals poured in during the afternoon. Day excursion traffic on Sundays and Bank Holiday Mondays was encouraged. Typical of these was a 1903 excursion from King's Cross to Yarmouth via Melton Constable, with a section to Weybourne, Sheringham and Cromer: twelve hours by the sea for 4s od (20p), 5s 6d (27½p) for those who wished to make a week of it. During the holiday season many more local excursions were run from resorts to other resorts or to inland places of interest. The Yarmouth herring season provided further traffic for fish workers' specials and fast fish trains in the autumn. Staffing at peaks was arranged by hiring staff for the season, laying them off in the winter and re-hiring them the following year as a regular arrangement. Such staff often had other casual work in the off-season, so this practice was not as drastic as it sounds.

Freight traffic, especially coal, benefitted from the joint ownership by two great coal-hauling railways. Coal traffic into the large Norwich City yards and smaller ones elsewhere in North Norfolk climbed to over 300,000 tons a year. Local agricultural traffic was carried and encouraged, but much of it was tied by mill location to the existing waterways, and did not transfer to the new railway. Some local houses built in North Walsham and in the north coast resorts after 1890, used bricks from the East Midlands, and this was but one of many local products partly superseded by cheaper products now more easily brought from other areas by rail. Fish traffic from Yarmouth to the Midlands was developed, as to a smaller extent was that from Cromer and Sheringham.

The 'Leicester' express was always the best-known of the M&GN trains, running throughout the year on weekdays until the closure in 1959. A few years before World War I it was scheduled to reach Melton Constable at 6.02 pm. In spite of its name it was in fact from both Birmingham and Leicester, with through coaches to Lowestoft, Norwich and

Cromer. The immaculate golden-ochre 4–4–0 heading the train of mixed teak and Midland red coaches pulled into the down side of the island platform. Norwich and Lowestoft passengers had a few minutes for a snack, or a visit to the toilet if they were travelling in a compartment coach. The Cromer portion was faster away. As that portion had to reverse, the locally-built 4–4–2 tank engine waiting would back down on to the rear of the express and take its three carriages away only four minutes after arrival. A little later the refreshed passengers in the Yarmouth and Lowestoft section started off eastwards, leaving the centre Norwich portion to make a more leisurely departure at 6.12 pm. After a short stop at Aylsham the now very light express crossed under the GER Cromer–Norwich line and climbed the sharp bank into North Walsham station. The advertised connection for Mundesley and Overstrand left from the GER station 150yd away, but was quite likely to be headed by an M&GN 4–4–0 tank of Yarmouth & North Norfolk vintage, indicating friendlier relations between the rivals, but not always to the passengers' convenience. The run to Yarmouth might include stops at Stalham and Ormesby if passengers from west of King's Lynn required either of them, otherwise it was a fast run to Yarmouth Beach, slowing-down only to exchange tablets at the end of each section of single track. The run alongside the beach near Caister was a foretaste of things to come for the holidaymaker. The final part of the journey started with a reversal at Yarmouth Beach followed by a climb on to the massive swing bridge across Breydon Water, often lit up by the setting sun, then across the Yarmouth Vauxhall–Norwich line, over the junctions and into Gorleston. Double lines and solidly-built stations marked this section, and high hopes were entertained of traffic development, so the express stopped at most of the little seaside stations to Lowestoft.

By the turn of the century, the sterility of competition and duplication of services dawned on the GER and M&GN,

so that when extensions from Mundesley to Cromer, and from Yarmouth to Lowestoft direct were mooted, they were as joint ventures, and for good measure, the North Walsham to Mundesley branch was added to what became the Norfolk & Suffolk Joint Committee lines. With co-operation established, the Great Eastern started to run a through London–Sheringham service in July 1906. The following year, the 'Norfolk Coast Express' was established, with sections for Sheringham, Cromer High and Mundesley. In spite of a very good, competitive train service, and easily accessible seaside resorts, the North Norfolk coast obstinately refused to develop a holiday trade on the scale of Yarmouth and Lowestoft. Although Lower Sheringham increased its population from 300 in 1881 to over 4,000 in 1901, it did not grow much larger, and Mundesley never topped a permanent population of 1,200 until after railway closure. The disappointment of Trimingham and Overstrand was even greater, as their populations hardly grew at all after the railway was built, and the hotels there were among the first to be converted to other purposes. By World War I one could say that the M&GN performed a useful local service, had established a modest new seaside area, and added to the fortunes of an existing one.

During the decade before World War I, the M&GN was in its prime. It made a modest living, the line was in good order, and engineering structures were adequate for the relatively small and light late-Victorian locomotives largely using it. Melton Constable works developed considerably in scope in these years. Locomotives of 0–6–0T and 4–4–2T designs were built in the period 1897–1909, and further 4–4–0s acquired. The task of keeping an ageing locomotive fleet in good order was by no means a light one, and the other rolling stock, often obtained second-hand from a wide variety of sources, needed constant attention.

Two generations of apprentices were trained at Melton, and Marriott noted with satisfaction that his training allowed them to command well-paid jobs both at home and abroad. The Railway Institute became the centre of improvement classes for engineering and running staff, making for a very self-contained system, with a character of its own. It was a family character as far as staffing was concerned: Marriott knew and cared for almost everybody. In mechanical and civil engineering, economy was the watchword, but the very best was obtained from equipment and structures within these limits. The turnout was always highly polished, the service personal.

Mr Marriott turned his inventive strain to concrete, and used his own patented machine in the concrete shop at Melton Constable to turn out such diverse articles as signal posts, cattle pens, gatehouses, nameboards, telegraph poles and prefabricated offices. Not only the home railway was supplied, but also the parent companies, other English companies and some for export to Ceylon (Sri Lanka.) The bulk of the raw material for this enterprise came from the quarries in the Holt-Kelling area, where extensive sidings adjoined the railway. Many of these products can still be seen today along the lineside, and a square-section post is still extant in the middle of Melton Constable works.

First World War I showed what a rural railway works could do when pressed. In addition to munitions work and maintenance of its own stock, Melton repaired seventy locomotives for the Midland Railway, over 500 wagons for the parent companies and built over seventy wagons for the Great Northern Railway. Overtime was worked willingly, although sometimes accompanied by Zeppelin raids.

Other mishaps occurred, the worst being the freak storm of 26–27 August 1912. Only the sections of line east of Fakenham were affected. Up to eight inches of rain fell in twenty-four hours, about one-third of the annual total in that part of England, and far more than the local drainage system could cope with. Slips of cuttings and embankments, especially in boulder clay areas, were frequent, culverts and bridges

Plates 5 and 6. The Southwold Railway. *Above:* A pre-1901 scene at Blythburgh station, with 2–4–0T *Halesworth*. *Below:* Halesworth station in 1938. *(A. R. Taylor collection)*

Plates 7 and 8. Studies in dereliction. *Above:* Horham station, Mid-Suffolk Light Railway, in 1973. *Below:* Shed at Blythburgh, Southwold Railway, in 1973. *(R. S. Joby)*

were destroyed, sections of track washed out and £20,000 of repair work had to be done. Although Marriott was suffering from food-poisoning at the time, he immediately set out in a horse brougham, which after a few yards was already floor-deep in water. A train was marooned at Aylesham for nearly five weeks. Seven-day working, with overtime, with assistance from King's Cross helped restore through services by 2 September via Cromer and Mundesley, and the following day the Melton Constable–Norwich line was re-opened to goods services.

The post-1918 scene saw the demise of the monopoly position of railways in inland transport. Within six months of the Armistice, buses were running from Norwich and Yarmouth to most of the towns served by the M&GN. The City station, in spite of its name, is a long walk from the commercial centre of Norwich, while many rural stations were up to two miles from the towns and villages they purported to serve, Weybourne and Reepham (Whitwell & Reepham Station) being good examples of this. The bus, of course, operated from the market square and stopped often at front doors, while in Norwich, passengers were set down outside the main stores.

Railway amalgamation had little effect at first on the M&GN. The shares owned by the Midland Railway passed to the successor London, Midland & Scottish Railway, while those of the Great Northern Railway passed to the London & North Eastern Railway, on 1 January 1923. The only apparent casualty was the King's Cross–Cromer Beach service, which was not resumed in the summer of 1923, as it competed directly with the ex-GER service. Bus competition, economic depression and rural depopulation all took their toll on traffic. Holiday resorts grew slowly in the inter-war period, but the section between Hemsby–Yarmouth and Lowestoft saw a hopeful experiment from 1925 in the launching of holiday camps. Holiday traffic was encouraged by the opening of halts at Cromer Links and Sidestrand on the

Cromer–Mundesley line in 1923 and 1936 respectively, while north of Yarmouth, halts were opened at Yarmouth Newtown, Caister Camp, California and Scratby in 1933. The 'Holiday Camps Express' was run for a new type of holidaymaker from 1934 until 1958, with a break caused by World War II. In the days before cars became the main means by which campers arrived, the rail service to the camps was very important, with the changeover of clientele taking place on summer Saturdays. The camps north of Yarmouth could not be reached by the direct line from Liverpool Street, so by using a unique route via Cambridge, Thetford, the Wensum Curve avoiding Norwich and then reversing at Antingham Road Junction, North Walsham, the express ran along the Mundesley branch connection into North Walsham Town station and on to Caister-on-Sea with stops at Potter Heigham, Hemsby and Caister Camp Halt. On a summer Saturday in the early 1950s the train left Liverpool Street just before 11.00 am. It consisted of ex-LNER bow-ended coaches in their 'blood-and-custard' livery, often headed by a rather austere black B1 4-6-0 locomotive. Families with mounds of luggage filled the compartments and settled down for the lengthy journey on the dusty plush seats. Only light refreshments were served, but sandwiches and flasks were the order of the day in any case. Stops were made for water as there were no troughs on the Cambridge line, but holiday anticipation overcame the tedium of the $3\frac{1}{2}$ hours to North Walsham. Passengers were sometimes disconcerted after passing through North Walsham (Main) and reversing to find themselves accelerating through North Walsham (Town) a few minutes later. The locomotive was now a standard British Railways Class 4MT 2-6-0, which dominated the final years of the M&GN. Broads visitors alighted at Potter Heigham where their boats awaited them, leaving the campers and their offspring to emerge further south after $4\frac{1}{2}$ hours' travel. A fortnight later the return trip started from Caister-on-Sea at 10.47 am and took a similar time on its journey. As express timings to Yarmouth came down to around three hours in the late 1950s the extra time seemed less attractive. Taxi services to the camps were used more frequently for the last few miles from South Town or Vauxhall stations, while more holiday-makers arrived in their own cars. Bradshaw's spring 1959 timetables forecast another season of holiday camps expresses, but this section of the M&GN was already closed.

A frequent service, at first operated by a steam railcar, and later by conventional means, operated between Yarmouth Beach and Stalham from 1933. Simultaneously, the fish traffic had halved, and the operating surplus reached only £3,556 in 1934, so that the days of semi-independence could not be long sustained. Such a surplus could not have supported major repairs and re-equipment, and as the subsequent LNER works programme showed, this was long overdue.

Operation was taken over by the LNER on 1 October 1936, which three months later transferred all locomotive operations to its Stratford works. Large numbers of LNER locomotives appeared and M&GN locomotives were rapidly scrapped, being both old and mostly non-standard. Traffic increased with the approach once more of war, as a dozen aerodromes were served, but after 1945 the decline set in again. Other functions of the Joint system were transferred to other LNER works and offices, eventually leaving only Melton Constable as a wagon sheet works. As the traffic declined, so the duplication of facilities with the GER lines became more apparent. When large numbers of holiday-makers deserted the railways in the 1950s for road transport, even the summer peak traffic could be accommodated by the one-time rival. The first casualty was the Cromer–Mundesley line. The long-awaited development of holiday traffic on this line still failed to materialise, large sections of beach remained closed because of mines laid in the war years, so closure was inevitable. Cromer High, poorly positioned on a ridge overlooking the town, closed to passengers in 1954, but kept its freight service until 1960. Only the tunnel of the N&SJR under the GER at Cromer High now remains. Further south, the link from Yarmouth Beach to Gorleston, on the Norfolk and Suffolk Joint was closed in 1953 at the end of the summer season. The impressive bridge across Breydon Water was not dismantled for a further decade. This closure resulted in the further loss of through traffic.

By the 1950s losses were beginning to spiral, with no sign of an end to the process. Freight traffic was transferred to road; the only trains running with good passenger loads were those on a summer Saturday and those carrying school children, hardly the basis for continued prosperity. On 28 February 1959 the Fakenham–Yarmouth section closed completely, apart from sidings at North Walsham made accessible by a short new line built in May 1958 for the last season of holiday camps expresses to Caister. Cromer–Norwich City was freight-only from Melton Constable southwards until a new connection was built in 1960 at Themelthorpe. Yarmouth Beach station is now the coach station, the Potter Heigham to Stalham section is the new by-pass, and a similar fate awaits the track-bed around North Walsham. The M&GN station at North Walsham was very well restored as a chapel for the Jehovah's Witnesses, but was pulled down in 1975 to make way for a sewage scheme. The typical criss-cross palings of the M&GN have also been preserved alongside the approach path. The section to Aylsham with its many level-crossings is a good place to see crossing-keepers' cottages, mostly of the same pattern, and only that at the Station Road crossing, North Walsham, has been destroyed, for road widening.

The opening of the Themelthorpe curve allowed the section northwards to be closed to all traffic. Guestwick station is still recognisable, and is a good example of a single-line station on this system. A further minor closure in 1960 was the lifting of the Newstead Lane–Runton West Junction curve. The embankment can still be clearly seen.

1964 saw the penultimate abandonments to date, with the complete closure to all traffic of the Melton Constable–Sheringham and North Walsham–Mundesley lines. By this time, rural East Anglia had reached the highest per capita car ownership in the country, so that trains on these lines had loads of half a dozen passengers or less in the middle of the day or in the evenings. The section Weybourne–Sheringham was retained for preservation by Central Norfolk Enterprises. Shareholders' specials are now being run over this section, and it was hoped to start a regular service in 1973 but this was delayed until 1975. Only Mundesley and Trimingham stations have been demolished on these lines; Weybourne and Sheringham are being preserved, Paston & Knapton station is an elegant private house, with the old trackbed now as a sunken garden. Melton Constable remains have been detailed above. The trackbed is easy to follow on both lines. They are both in hilly, attractive country, with deep cuttings and high embankments, unlike so many other lines in Norfolk. The Mundesley branch now has a gas condensate pipeline buried under the former track, to serve the railhead at North Walsham with condensate from Bacton. The old Kelling Heath ballast, which is still in position, is so sterile that almost nothing grows, so dry-shod walking is easy at any time of the year.

The final abandonment was from Lenwade to Norwich City in 1970. The track is down to within 400yd of the Attlebridge yard, but trains stop now at the concrete products factory at Lenwade, which is the present *raison d'être* of the line. Norwich City has been largely stripped, and the site of the platforms and their ersatz war-time booking-office has disappeared under the Inner Link road scheme. The stations and attractive A-frame bridges at Drayton, Hellesdon and Mile Cross are still extant, and may be preserved as part of a linear park.

Now that the railways have nearly gone, North-East Norfolk is at last showing signs of fast growth again, too late for a restoration of comprehensive railway facilities, but possibly adequate to retain what is left. Melton Constable and North Walsham are the places which best repay visits, while Sheringham and Weybourne give a whiff of what has been preserved.

CHAPTER 3

North-West Norfolk

Apart from the line from Dereham to Fakenham, which is still open, North-West Norfolk benefitted little from the Railway Mania. The only moderate-sized town other than Fakenham in the mid-nineteenth century was Wells-next-the-Sea. Wells was a locally important but declining port, unable to take ships of increasing size, yet it served the estates of Lord Leicester and provided a valuable service importing coal and exporting farm produce. A series of lines from Wells Harbour and town to Blakeney, Fakenham and King's Lynn was planned in the 1840s but it was not until 1857 that the first line was opened, that from Wells to Fakenham. The Wells & Fakenham Railway was built as a separate railway, largely due to the efforts of Lord Leicester and Norfolk Railway directors. Far from revitalising Wells, the decline of the port continued despite the addition of a harbour branch three years later. The Wells & Fakenham Railway was worked by the Eastern Counties Railway in its usual slipshod manner, but on incorporation into the Great Eastern Railway in 1862 it became part of an important north–south line focused on London's growing food markets.

The next line to come to Wells was the West Norfolk Junction Railway from Heacham, which opened throughout in August 1866. This line entered Wells via a very sharp curve, so that the line almost reversed direction. For nearly a century Wells became a very busy terminal for so small a place, with a dozen or more passenger trains a day, as well as the trundle around to the quay by goods trains. The

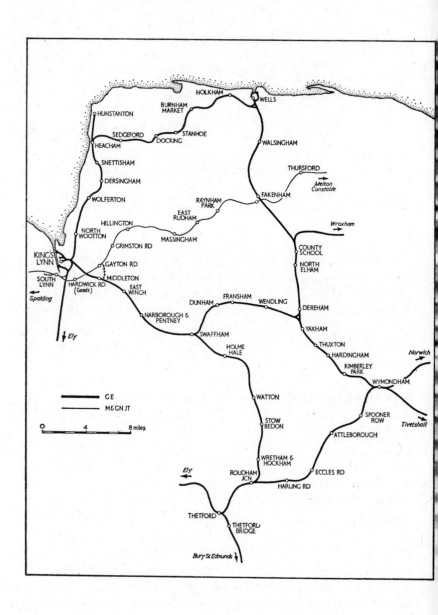

HUNSTANTON
SEDGEFORD
HEACHAM
SNETTISHAM
DERSINGHAM
WOLFERTON
HILLINGTON
NORTH
WOOTTON
GRIMSTON RD
KINGS
LYNN
GAYTON RD
SOUTH
LYNN
MIDDLETON
HARDWICK RD
(Goods)
EAST
WINCH
Spalding
Ely
NARBOROUGH &
PENTNEY
MASSINGHAM
EAST
RUDHAM
RAYNHAM
PARK
HOLKHAM
BURNHAM
MARKET
STANHOE
DOCKING
WELLS
WALSINGHAM
THURSFORD
Melton
Constable
FAKENHAM
COUNTY
SCHOOL
NORTH
ELHAM
Wroxham
DUNHAM
FRANSHAM
WENDLING
DEREHAM
YAXHAM
THUXTON
HARDINGHAM
KIMBERLEY
PARK
SWAFFHAM
HOLME
HALE
WATTON
STOW
BEDON
WRETHAM &
HOCKHAM
ROUDHAM
JCN
HARLING RD
ECCLES RD
ATTLEBOROUGH
SPOONER
ROW
WYMONDHAM
Norwich
Tivetshall
THETFORD
THETFORD
BRIDGE
Bury St Edmunds
Ely

GE
M&GN JT

0   4   8 miles

station was substantial and had sheltered platforms. The busy mill beside the station wafted the smell of animal feed-stuffs to mix with odours of smoke, steam and hot oil from the locomotive, and the fishy smells of the boxes of 'Stiffkey Blues' which were loaded into the guards' vans of trains connecting with expresses further south. Wells was the epitome of the small port station. The shellfish boxes and sacks dripped 'fish juice', but this caused little trouble until the changeover to diesel railcars came. Then the chemical action on the working parts caused frequent breakdowns until special leak-proof trays were developed at Norwich sheds to overcome the problem.

Nearby Walsingham was the other station of note. It was not until the 1930s that the shrines developed as centres of major pilgrimage. The Anglicans, under Father Hope Patten, had (and still have) their shrine in the village, the Roman Catholics a separate shrine alongside the Wells–Fakenham line a mile south of Walsingham station, where trains were sometimes stopped to detrain numerous pilgrims. The trains then ran forward to Wells for engine turning and carriage cleaning. Very long trains from the Midlands and elsewhere arrived for important feasts. It is appropriate that the station at Walsingham is now itself a shrine for a third Christian group; three Russian Orthodox monks have crowned the station building with golden domes and hold services in the old booking hall.

The Lynn & Hunstanton and the West Norfolk Junction Railway from Heacham to Wells were completed on 3 October 1862 and 17 August 1866 respectively at a time when North-West Norfolk started to attract holidaymakers in large numbers. The line was built cheaply thanks to the gifts and investment of Hamon Le Strange of Hunstanton, who also promoted a brand-new seaside resort, the first railway age resort in Norfolk, on his estate at New Hunstanton. The Lynn & Hunstanton Railway was an instant financial success, encouraging the building of the Heacham to Wells line which unlike most Norfolk railways paid dividends, but was never as profitable as the former.

The use of the Lynn & Hunstanton Railway to Wolferton for the wedding special of the Prince of Wales (later King Edward VII) focused public attention on the line on 10 March 1863. The locomotive, Sinclair 2-2-2 No 284, was painted cream for the occasion, decorated with roses, and its chimney garlanded. As the Prince settled down to the life of a Norfolk country gentleman, he made the Royal waiting-room at Wolferton a focal point on the Sandringham estates. It was used for luncheon parties during shoots, and the drive up to Sandringham House from Wolferton was through banks of glorious rhododendrons which came right down to the line.

Royal trains mostly used St Pancras as their London terminal during the nineteenth century, as Liverpool Street was in the City of London—by tradition the City was barred to Royalty except on special occasions. The royal trains were routed via the Tottenham & Hampstead line on to the GER Cambridge line. At Wolferton there were special sidings for the coaches and the line from King's Lynn to Wolferton was doubled in 1898, Wolferton station being rebuilt in mock Tudor style around the Prince of Wales' waiting-room.

Special trains continued to be a feature of the Lynn & Hunstanton. The twenty-first birthday of Prince Albert on 3 June 1886 brought Sayers Circus Special to Wolferton. After the performance one of the elephants proved difficult to reload, so an employee tied it to a lamp-post which it promptly uprooted, going on to demolish the station gates before calmly walking into its truck.

Spick-and-span locomotives were always a feature of the Royal trains, from the cream Sinclair single to the immaculate blue oil-burning T19 which hauled the wedding train of the Duke of York (later King George V) on 6 July 1893 and to the latter-day apple-green Claud Hamilton 4-4-0s of LNER days.

The turn-round at King's Lynn was as smart as the locomotives. Typically a Royal train left St Pancras at 12.20 pm,
arriving at King's Lynn at 2.32 pm, departing three minutes
later for the ten-minute run to Wolferton.

The Lynn & Hunstanton line also served thousands of
humbler citizens each year with holiday trains and excursions
to Hunstanton, where long island platforms could take
excursion trains with up to a thousand people aboard and
discharge them straight on to the promenade and pier. For
a brand-new resort the location of the station was ideal,
unlike Cromer or two of the Yarmouth stations. Long-stay
holidaymakers came and left on Saturdays, while the trippers
mainly came on Sundays in a constant stream of trains at
ten-minute intervals. Especially busy times were major works
outings from the Midlands and North when half-a-dozen or
more trains arrived within an hour, calling for fine timing
on a single line.

The 'Sandringham Hotel' at the end of the platform was
nicely placed for those who detested long walks and cabs.
Their appetite for the resort had been whetted by the
journey alongside the Wash where the sea appears to come
nearer and nearer the train the nearer to Hunstanton one
got, as the train threaded its way between mud flats and
dry land.

Heacham Junction was where one usually changed trains
for Wells, although day-tripper trains went through from
King's Lynn to Wells. The line was radically different in
scenery from the Hunstanton line, travelling through rolling
chalk country until Burnham Market (alighting point for
Nelson's birthplace) and then across drained salt marshes with
dunes to seaward and Holkham Park on the other side. The
stations, such as Stanhoe and Docking largely preserved as
private residences complete with nameboards, were among
the most delightful in East Anglia both architecturally and
florally. This line was also one of the last on which one
could travel in gas-lit clerestory coaches hauled by Victorian

locomotives right up to the end of passenger traffic in 1952.

For many years up to the mid-1950s, North-West Norfolk and Claud Hamilton locomotives were inseparably linked. Whether it were Royal trains, Hunstanton expresses or humble all-stations locals, these sterling locomotives did the job admirably. Their versatility ensured them a lengthy old age, though cut short by the arrival of diesel railcars in 1955.

The Midland & Great Northern Joint line from King's Lynn to Fakenham and on to Melton Constable was the fastest section of that redoubtable route. Originally an independent branch line from King's Lynn to Fakenham, this joined forces with the Yarmouth & North Norfolk Railway before either was opened for traffic. After much scheming, and trouble with Bills in Parliament, they managed to combine to give a through line right across Norfolk from east to west, with links to the Midlands and the North via the Lynn Loop line which avoided the King's Lynn GER terminal. Between Grimston Road and Raynham Park where the line doubled, some of the fastest single-line working ever seen was made possible by the use of Whitaker automatic tablet exchanges. The King's Cross to Cromer express before World War I had to be fast in order to compete with the GER expresses which ran over the shorter and much faster route from Liverpool Street to Cromer. The timing of the best M&GNJR train from King's Cross to Cromer via Peterborough at the end of the nineteenth century was just under four hours, with a non-stop run from Peterborough to Melton Constable, but this was exceptional and it was not until after 1908 and the general introduction of the Whitaker apparatus that most trains were speeded-up over the single-line sections. The apparatus was invented only three years before on the remarkably-similar Somerset & Dorset Joint Railway. Attempts to exchange tablets manually led to injury or loss and slowing-down at stations was a great hindrance to the dense train operations of summer weekends. The catching

48

apparatus was like a giant clothes peg which caught the tablet in its jaws at speeds of up to 50mph while yielding the tablet for the preceding section to the catching apparatus. The fireman swung the locomotive's apparatus out before reaching an exchanging station and retrieved the tablet after metallic clicks indicated a successful exchange. About one in seventy were unsuccessful; stopping and retrieval was fairly rare but costly in time when it did occur.

The section from King's Lynn to Melton Constable originally started from the GER station and ran in a loop via Bawsey before crossing the estates of the original directors of the Lynn & Fakenham Railway, the greatest of whom was the Marquis Townshend. This line was abandoned when the Lynn Loop was built in 1885, being opened the following New Year's Day. The through route from Yarmouth and Norwich to the Midlands had been greatly hindered until then both by almost continuous single line and by constant reversals. The King's Lynn reversal was made difficult by GER hostility and a high rent. It was in fact cheaper to raise the money to build the Lynn Loop and pay interest on it rather than continue to pay large sums to the GER.

While the main traffic from 1883 was through freight and passengers from the Midlands and North, there was a quieter rural traffic which could be observed by alighting at a country station and talking to the staff, who usually had time to spend answering questions between frantic bouts of activity when trains were in the station. The booking office was a treasure house for the inquisitive railway enthusiast right up to the closure of the M&GN. A comprehensive stock of tickets and labels to everywhere on the system was held in even very small booking offices and the ticket sales books had pages for stations on planned lines which were never built, such as the Blakeney branch. As original stocks had been more than adequate, and demand over the years very low, it was possible to buy advertising tickets of M&GN origin at Fakenham twenty years after the LNER took over operation,

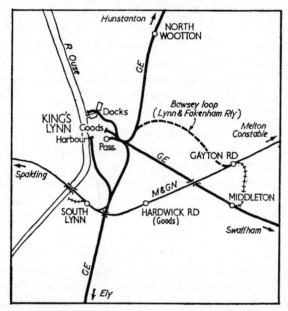

while one could have one's luggage labelled with Eastern & Midlands or even Lynn & Fakenham labels if one's destination were unusual enough.

Chats to the goods clerk generally elicited the full economic situation of the district, the quality of crops being despatched was noted and commented upon while consignments of pheasants told him the kind of season it had been. The great event of the day was the arrival of the pick-up goods train, often headed by a stolid Ivatt o-6-o maid-of-all work, which on a summer Saturday would be hauling a Yarmouth special. The shunter performed miracles of dexterity with his clanging, unwieldy charges, perfectly co-ordinating manoeuvres with the footplate crew who interpreted his every gesture accurately amid the hiss of steam and grinding of brake blocks. All too soon the performance would be over, the new wagons awaiting unloading, the train re-assembled and chugging slowly off, the guard's van accelerating with a convulsive lurch.

Most stations east of King's Lynn had crossing-keepers who were on duty almost round-the-clock at peak periods. Before World War II they were often railway pensioners or invalid staff who were content with their meagre pensions of a few shillings a week and a line-side vegetable garden. The keen gardeners often extended their plots further and further alongside the track with the knowing connivance of inspectors who were grateful for the occasional cauliflower from a productive garden. With the aid of a wife the gate could be manned continuously, three of four calls in an hour being not uncommon at weekends. The railway cottage was better than most in the village and there were other compensations as a railway servant—the lumps of coal that rolled off the tenders of locomotives whose drivers they knew, the opportunity to be the first to spot a pheasant knocked down by a train, and innumerable other little perks which are now part of railway lore and history. One location near a level-crossing was famous for its horseradish crop on the sides of a cutting. The keeper acted as unofficial harvester when intervals between trains permitted, and the crop was passed along the line by stopping trains. Such a system of crossings, while saving much capital initially, made this line in particular a target for closure when full rates of pay had to be given to crossing-keepers, plus many hours of overtime each week. Passenger trains ceased on 28 February 1959 but goods trains continued from King's Lynn to East Rudham for a further nine years. The latter station is particularly worth seeing as it still has crane and goods shed complete and largely unvandalised.

The focus for the Lynn & Fakenham section of the M&GN was South Lynn with a large locomotive shed and a branch to King's Lynn GER station, the train for which was hauled until the early 1930s by one of the original 4-4-0 tanks. South Lynn shed was being rebuilt when the M&GN was axed on 28 February 1959, vindicating the foreboding of a signalman who told the author that a certain sign of impending closure was the arrival of the painters and decorators at the station after years of absence. Coincidence perhaps—but he had a point about lack of co-ordination.

The main junction of the remaining lines in North-West Norfolk was Swaffham, a small market town, pleasant, unpretentious, and far from dynamic but the scene of yet another attempt to form a through route from rural Norfolk to busier places. Originally the East Anglian Railway had built a line by easy stages through Swaffham from King's Lynn to Dereham, where it joined the Norfolk Railway. King's Lynn was the natural outlet for the produce of the district. The coming of the railways allowed towns to enlarge their economic hinterlands, and while the instrument of Lynn's imperialism in the 1840s was the East Anglian Railway, it was not until the 1860s that Bury St Edmunds' brewers and bankers conceived the plan of a series of lines into the heart of Norfolk via Thetford and Watton, using part of the Norfolk Railway between Thetford Bridge and Roudham Junction. Financial difficulties were such that Charles Parkes of the GER was called in to help, one of his first (though by no means last) operations to save an over-extended scheme. Through services from the Watton line operated over the triangular junction at Thetford for a short period after opening and it was possible to avoid all the major GER bottlenecks by routing traffic onwards via Long Melford to Marks Tey and London. Almost immediately, however, this was abandoned as a through route and the line from Thetford to Swaffham was operated as a minor cross-country link. The owning companies were a continuing trial to the GER and their shareholders, but one of the poorest parts of Norfolk had the benefits of rail travel.

In the years before World War I the Breckland developed as a battleground for military manoeuvres. In the early days, horse vans were an important part of the military trains, with open trucks for the artillery. When the Territorials came for their summer camps, Thetford Bridge and

Plates 9 and 10. The Mildenhall branch. *Above:* Exning Road Halt, with Class F4 2–4–2T No 67239. The primitive GER halt is well exemplified in this illustration. *Below:* Manpower alone turns Class E4 2–4–0 No 62785 on the turntable at Mildenhall. *(Dr I. C. Allen)*

Plates 11 and 12. Big engines. *Above:* At South Lynn shed, M&GNR, in the mid-1950s. *Below:* Class B17 4–6–0 No 61622 *Alnwick Castle* doubles as goods train locomotive and shunter on the Stour Valley line at Cavendish in 1955. *(Dr I. C. Allen)*

Wretham & Hockham stations were indeed busy, often day and night. Tanks and armoured vehicles replaced the picturesque cavalry and horse-artillery between the wars, while in the late 1930s many airfields were built in Breckland, with the one at Watton almost alongside the line. The new breed of conscript was more affluent than his predecessor and eager to go home for even 36- or 48-hour leaves. The precious buff slip which promised brief freedom and allowed reduced rail fares was shown at Watton and Holme Hale booking offices and Friday night trains were usually full when there was a lull in operations or in the years of National Service after World War II. The late Sunday service was run almost exclusively for servicemen returning from leave. Between these bouts of frantic activity the station staff at Watton had time to become the best-known topiarists on the Eastern Region. The Watton line was regularly a line used by E4 locomotives, a sure sign after 1930 of being a backwater, but also making it a mecca for railway enthusiasts.

The Dereham to Lynn line had pretensions of being more important despite being single. Claud Hamilton 4–4–0 locomotives increasingly migrated here as their main line duties were taken over by Sandringhams in the 1930s. There was an alternative service from Norwich to King's Lynn via the M&GN which was faster at certain times of the day. The pace was always sedate via Swaffham, the fastest train barely averaged 30mph, only ran twice-weekly, and omitted but three stations on its leisurely schedule. The slow tempo of rural Norfolk lines was endearing to some but those with urgent business bought cars and the line linking Norwich with the main town in West Norfolk atrophied and closed on 9 September 1968. Today the thousand square miles of North-West Norfolk has no railways apart from goods spurs to Fakenham and Middleton sand quarries, yet only twenty years ago the M&GN and the Lynn & Hunstanton together could muster a hundred trains a day between them, often with ten coaches in a train.

CHAPTER 4

The Fens

The Fens once formed a vast inland gulf of marshland dotted with islands such as Ely, Thorney and Ramsey. The area was largely drained between the seventeenth and early nineteenth centuries, thus permitting farming on the rich peat and silt soils in what had formerly been marshes. Vast quantities of cereals, roots, potatoes and vegetables were harvested, to which were added fruit in the late nineteenth century and sugar beet in the twentieth century. Apart from the 'islands', the landscape is totally flat except where the rivers have been embanked to prevent flooding. On gradient profiles of Fen railways it is only river crossings which provide any relief from the dead level. This is not to say that the Fens are a monotonous countryside either for landscape or railways. Far from it; many of the towns and villages are gems, well worth visits, the arching sky is ever varied and the great sweeps of crops, carpets of flowers around Spalding in the spring, or orchards heavy with fruit in the autumn have a magic all of their own.

George Stephenson had discovered the techniques of building railways across marshes in 1829, so that when Fenland railways were built in the 1840s few constructional problems were encountered, the main problem being which of the multiplicity of planned lines were to be constructed.

The basic main lines of the Fens were those of the Eastern Counties Railway from Cambridge to Peterborough, built as part of George Hudson's grandiose plans for a line to York, and those radiating from King's Lynn, built by that pauper amongst East Anglian lines the East Anglian Railway to Ely via Downham Market, and the loop from Magdalen Road to March via Wisbech. Of these only the line from Magdalen Road to Wisbech has closed. Later lines have been less fortunate in this respect, being built either to compete with existing lines or to fill gaps in the system and serve minor centres which have subsequently turned to lorries as their prime goods movers. The lines which formed the Western Division of the Midland & Great Northern Joint system were built between 1858 and 1866, giving the partners access to King's Lynn and later forming an essential link in the wayward but lovable cross-country line from the Midlands to the East Coast. Most interesting of all were the various attempts to make cheap railways to serve agricultural districts, such as the Wisbech & Upwell Tramway, the Wissington lines, the Benwick goods spur and the purely private estate railway on the edge of the Fens at Edenham.

The M&GN lines ran from King's Lynn westwards to Sutton Bridge, crossing The Great Ouse by a conventional bridge at South Lynn and using a road-and-rail swing bridge to cross the Nene at Sutton Bridge. This busy section was doubled during the great rebuilding of the system in the 1890s. The bridge was known as the Cross Keys Bridge and now functions as a road bridge only. Sutton Bridge station was on a very sharp curve just off the main road, and served as a very busy despatch point for vegetables, fruit, flowers and other produce. The staff really cared about the passengers, few as they were in later years. The waiting-room was immaculate, the most highly-polished that the writer ever saw, the table had a mirror finish and was covered at one end with neat piles of magazines for passenger use. The lines then diverged westwards towards Peterborough and Spalding across seemingly limitless hedgeless fields, past stations with strange names such as Counter Drain and Twenty until the terra firma of the Jurassic limestones was reached on the other side of this unique region. This was high-speed territory

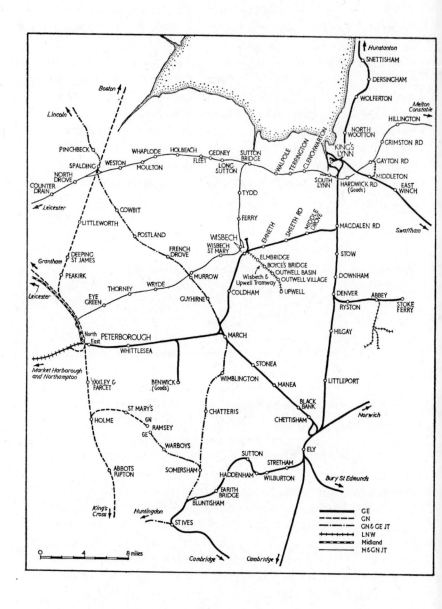

for the endless stream of excursions and other specials which streamed across the Fens every summer weekend for so many years, bearing tens of thousands of holidaymakers to the East Coast in a single day. They sometimes operated around the clock, straining railway resources to the limit.

Somehow a heavy fruit traffic was also despatched during the summer. The queue of fruit growers' traps and farmers' carts at the sidings was often lengthy, especially when trucks were in short supply. Heavy wicker baskets were piled high into covered vans destined for all parts of industrial England. A sturdy shire horse moved the vans about the sidings at wayside stations, well-practised in his job and not afraid of the wheezing pick-up goods engine when it arrived daily. Other traffic which kept this section busy included the brick traffic around Peterborough, with concomitant inward coal traffic, long through coal trains from the Midlands and North to Norwich and Yarmouth, and fitted fish trains speeding in the opposite direction.

In this flat yet attractive landscape level-crossings were a very frequent feature, no less than fifty-five of them on the Western Section of the M&GN, each with its own little barge-gabled cottage, the most recent of them made of concrete from Melton Constable, often run by a retired railwayman and his wife who during the summer took it in turns to keep the crossing manned round the clock in return for a pittance.

The Wisbech & Upwell Tramway was of a very different nature, one of the first attempts to provide a cheaply-built public railway in a rural area, operated by steam. It ran for the most part between a canal and a public road. The line was experimental in that the Great Eastern Railway was supported by the Board of Trade in building the line in order to bring rail transport to areas that were uneconomic to serve with a full-scale railway. Construction costs at £2,284 per mile were a quarter of those of a typical branch line of the period, while most of the land was bought on reasonable terms. Three canal bridges were the only engineering features; no fencing was required for most of the length, and lineside structures were small and cheap. The line initially opened to Outwell on 20 August 1883, continuing to Upwell on 3 September 1884. Extensions were planned, but the Great Eastern wished to judge the success of the line before committing itself further. Soon after opening 3,000 passengers a week were being carried, together with 600 tons of goods, later swelled by coal traffic to Outwell where the coal was transferred to barges for servicing the pumping engines on the Fenland waterways. The traffic in vegetables and fruit grew steadily and passenger traffic was denser than on most East Anglian branch lines until buses came after World War I, making an early and easy conquest of this line which had greater speed restrictions than almost any other.

Almost all train operations on the Wisbech & Upwell were different from those on a more conventional railway. At Wisbech East station was a specially low platform. The train which greeted passengers changing at Wisbech consisted of a small tank locomotive shaped like a guard's van, but also equipped with a cowcatcher at either end, a bell atop the roof and skirting covering the wheels and motion to prevent the movement frightening horses, so it was said. More prosaically the law required that 'the machinery shall be concealed from view at all points above four inches from the level of the rails and all fire used on such engines shall be concealed from view'. The sound of Victorian moralising was very evident in the drafting. The carriages were of the tramway type, with balconies at each end and a gangway of the drawbridge type connecting the carriages for the guard to proceed from one to the other while en route at the maximum speed of 12mph, reduced to 8mph at Elm Road Crossing and New Common Bridge and right down to 4mph through facing points and at Outwell when crossing the road. To ensure compliance, the locomotives were fitted with governors which cut off steam at a speed of 12mph. Mixed

trains were run at times but passenger traffic was quite heavy
before 1927, and a maximum of nine passenger coaches was
permitted.

Four-wheeled carriages only were used in the first year
of operation, but a pair of bogie coaches which later went
to the Kelvedon & Tollesbury Light Railway was introduced
a year later. Thomas Worsdell designed the original tram
locomotives, 0–4–0 tanks classified Y6 by the LNER, and
ten were eventually built to work on this line and on dock
lines previously horse-worked. Heavier trains demanded
larger locomotives so an 0–6–0 tank with outside cylinders
was designed by James Holden in 1903 and twelve of these
were built up to 1921. The locomotives were not only shaped
like guards' vans, they were also painted like them, teak
under the Great Eastern, and brown with black lower parts
after the 1923 amalgamation. Two other unique vehicles
were used, a special luggage van later transferred to the
Elsenham & Thaxted Light Railway, and a guard's van.
Ordinary goods vehicles were used for freight services as most
traffic was transferred to the main lines at Wisbech.

The little teak coloured train, apparently headed by a
smoking guard's van, which awaited passengers in pre-World
War I Wisbech, ambled along the line towards King's Lynn
before turning sharply southwards after a third of a mile.
The main road was crossed at the level, guarded by a signalman with a red flag. Thenceforth the train could be stopped
by intending passengers flagging it down at any point as well
as the fixed and rather frequent official stopping places. New
Common Bridge was hump-backed and very difficult to cross
when the train was heavy and the rails wet or frosty. Elm
Bridge, Boyce's Bridge and Outwell all had goods sidings,
so the little train had to slow to a crawl to negotiate the
facing points.

Leaving Outwell the line continued on reserved track to
the large depot at Upwell where there were nine goods
sidings as well as passenger facilities. Between six and eight

return passenger trips a day were run until the end of passenger services on New Year's Eve, 1927. Despite a 39 minute journey for the 5 miles 79 chains, it was faster than walking or even by pony and trap unless the pony was whipped unmercifully. Buses changed this however, and delivered their pasengers at the market instead of half-a-mile away, so that the Wisbech & Upwell Tramway was the first branch line in Norfolk to lose its passenger service, apart from the abandoned Bawsey Loop and the private Scole Railway. Goods traffic was thriving, however.

In 1930 a double-ended Sentinel 100hp geared steam locomotive was introduced, but consumed too much water for the tramway's limited resources and was later sent to the Yarmouth Quay lines. The original steam tram engines resumed their long-held monopoly and retained it until 1952 when a Drewry diesel shunter complete with tramway skirts was introduced, but it took a year of trial and error before steam was entirely ousted and two diesels, with a new shed built for them at Wisbech, finally commenced their reign which lasted until final closure on 23 May 1966. As late as the 1950s there were eight goods departures a day from Upwell in the fruit season and during the potato harvest.

Despite its success in traffic terms, the Wisbech & Upwell experiment was not repeated with later lines. The Light Railways Act of 1896 allowed more conventional railways to be built more cheaply and to use 'normal', if rather light, locomotives and rolling stock. The line from Three Horseshoes Junction to Benwick was a goods-only light railway from the beginning, starting from a junction in open country and running straight across the Fens to the hamlet of Benwick. Sidings for loading produce were found at roughly one-mile intervals with trains running to suit the traffic. Crossing as it did the richest Fenland it concentrated solely on coal and produce and was closed on 13 July 1964 after sixty-six years of useful and unobtrusive service.

A whole system of light railways was built from 1906

onwards around Wissington and Methwold, joining the Stoke Ferry branch at Abbey. These lines were goods-only, followed circuitous routes to serve the maximum area, and after the building of the Wissington Sugar Beet Factory in 1925 served as one of the main hauliers of intensively-grown sugar beet. Eighteen miles of track were eventually opened, operated by British Sugar Corporation o–6–oTs and working most intensively between September and January. The lack of good all-weather roads made the Wissington lines essential far longer than similar lines elsewhere and the system was taken over by the Ministry of Agriculture as a wartime measure in 1941, followed by purchase in 1947, finally closing south of the sugar factory in 1957. Five locomotives were used, based at the sugar factory, indicating the heavy seasonal peak in traffic. Such a system is more reminiscent of Ireland than England and was an illustration of what could have been achieved elsewhere with lightly-laid lines focusing on a specialised processing plant. Upgrading of lines to carry passengers was not essential; the main element that needed reducing in the Edwardian rural economy was transport costs if the English farmer was to compete with imports and with as little capital outlay as possible. In this the Wissington system came near to perfection.

Another and much earlier private venture was the Edenham Railway on the western fringe of the Fens. This steam-operated line ran from the Great Northern Railway to the estate of Lord Willoughby de Eresby at Edenham, a distance of four miles, and was built as early as 1856. There were two very small o–4–o tank locomotives and a pair of ex-LNWR coaches running on a very rough permanent way. The locomotives deteriorated under the rough riding and handling they received and by 1872 they were beyond repair, after which date the line ceases to appear in Bradshaw. However, goods traffic continued with horse traction until the 1880s when the line itself seems to have been in need of complete overhaul. The building of the new M&GN line from Bourne to Saxby used part of the route and destroyed the formation in 1894, but also provided better services for the district, thus obviating the need to renew the original line. Estate railways have been a feature of several parts of the British scene and we meet another at Scole in Norfolk, but none of the great landlords of East Anglia had one built although many were very interested in railway affairs and were instrumental in having lines built in their locality.

Most of the farmers' lines in the Fens were light in construction and late in completion but one line defied this pattern, the Wisbech, St Ives & Cambridge Junction Railway whose Bill passed through Parliament in 1846; the line was quickly built in an almost straight line across the Fens, opening from March to Wisbech on 3 May 1847 and from St Ives to March nine months later. None of the procrastination, bankruptcies and other toils experienced by so many other rural lines proposed by and constructed for local landowners attended the genesis of this line, which was taken over successively by the Eastern Counties Railway in 1848 before completion, by the Great Eastern Railway in 1862, and then the March to St Ives section was vested in the GN&GE Joint Railway in 1882. As a means of avoiding Ely, which at that period was greatly congested with traffic from six directions, the March, St Ives to Cambridge route had much to recommend it. Local traffic was largely agricultural before the Doncaster to March line was opened, but thereafter a cavalcade of coal trains moved from the East Midlands towards east London, lengthy, slow-moving but immensely profitable to the GER. As ever more powerful o–6–o goods tender locomotives appeared from Stratford works so the trains grew longer. Passenger traffic was light, as only market towns and villages were served and through passenger trains were few. Expresses usually used the Ely line, as that city was the great interchange station for through lines of the GER in northern East Anglia.

Somersham was the only junction station between St Ives and March. From the dead level and straight through line a meandering branch curved around the contours of the great Fen 'island' of Ramsey, serving Warboys and Ramsey. Although promoted locally, and taking an inordinate time to build in comparison with the line to which it was joined, it became part of the GN&GE Joint Railway. The original intention was to join it to the GNR branch from Holme to Ramsey, a line in which the GER had a controlling interest but which was operated by the GNR. This was never built and, given that neither of the Ramsey branches was convenient for passengers, it was not surprising that the Ramsey to Somersham branch closed to regular passengers on 22 September 1930, its erstwhile rival on 6 October 1947. Occasional passenger traffic continued in the form of annual excursions to Clacton via Cambridge and Colchester. Up to five hundred people travelled on pre-war excursions from Ramsey (East), a sizeable proportion of the town population. For an hour before departure mothers with large wicker baskets on one arm, leading expectant children with the other hand trooped towards the station, father ambling along behind. Countryfolk took everything needed for the whole day out, leading to complaints of stinginess from seaside traders. Fares for the family amounted to a week's wages for father, so this was a day to be savoured.

The busiest time for all the Fen lines was from June to October, although the planting of sugar-beet in the 1920s evened the load somewhat and increased the amount of winter work. Coal trucks were mostly dealt with by the merchants, so that the railway staff did not find this traffic such a burden. Sutton was the central station on the line from Ely to St Ives and one of many stations throughout the Fens which would serve to illustrate the annual pattern of traffic in the inter-war period. A seasonal phenomenon was the arrival of pickers for the various crops with which the railway dealt. Nowadays students and travelling folk do most of the work, but then the pickers were mostly towns-people, often Londoners taking working holidays, together with the local unemployed, tramps and gypsies in horse-drawn caravans. Special trains of the most elderly vehicles were used, usually compartment non-corridor stock which had the dual advantage of greater capacity and of being easier to watch for damage. The pickers brought huge mounds of baggage, ancient suitcases bursting at the seams, bedding wrapped in counterpanes as a bundle, wicker baskets and great stone bottles plus cooking utensils. The farmers brought carts, covered horse-vans and trucks down to the station to meet this motley crew of women, children and a few men, who were then bumped and jolted away to shacks and temporary cabins dotted around the orchards and straw-berry fields.

The key marshalling yards supplying trucks for the produce, assembling trains and providing locomotives were March and Ely. These nerve-centres of the Fens despatched trainloads of empty trucks and vans to the lines radiating from them. Along the lines, not only the stations but also sidings with no stations were busy all day long, with any-thing from a dozen to fifty trucks being loaded by hand. Station yards were full of the typical Fen tumbrils and tipping carts, the patient horses being watered or snuffling in their nosebags while awaiting their turns to empty the carts. Sometimes, and too often in the opinion of Fenland farmers, the number of vans was inadequate and the last of the full carts would be sent away to return on the following day. This was particularly annoying when the crops were perishable. Using the railway was an art to be judged finely. If one picked crops till late then there was a strong chance of being turned away! Rainy days were another hazard. Picking of strawberries often stopped as fruit was damaged, yet the station yards had empty wagons and if usage was low then it increased the chances of fewer wagons being sent subsequently.

So busy were Fen stations by mid-June that more staff were drafted in from suburban areas and elsewhere, which were then at their slackest. Permanent way staff and others were also employed to load fruit at the height of the despatch season; everything that could be was dropped in an attempt to meet the mid-afternoon deadline when the wagons were picked-up. Earlier a posse of locomotives set out from March and Ely in all directions to bring back long trainloads of produce, which were then transferred to the sidings to be sorted according to final destination. After Whitemoor yards at March were rebuilt in 1931 this was greatly expedited and there was more certainty that Fenland fruit would reach market the day following picking.

Sugar-beet kept the Fenland railways busy with short-haul goods trains from September until late January or early February. The British Sugar Corporation factories at King's Lynn, Wissington and Ely took most of their deliveries by rail and water. The same sidings, scented with strawberries in summer, now looked dourly grey and misty in the chill dawn as steaming horses plodded towards the trucks; there was mud everywhere and farm lads who were content to wait an hour or two in mid-summer were unwilling to chill themselves in the dank air, with no more than a sack around their shoulders as extra protection in the exposed position atop the cart.

The best route to see the remains of abandoned Fenland railways is probably a figure-of-eight, joinable anywhere en route but for the purposes of illustration starting at King's Lynn. The main road westwards runs almost parallel with the former M&GN main line, but diversions have to be made to see stations en route before Sutton Bridge, where one crosses the former road-rail swing bridge which is now all road. One can proceed westwards as far as Spalding, Bourne or Edenham before turning south to Peterborough, then turning alongside the M&GN line go to Wisbech, which is worth a long stop both for richness in remains and for the town itself, the nearest thing in East Anglia to a Dutch canalside town. From Wisbech the Wisbech & Upwell line can be followed, continuing to Downham Market, Wissington and Stoke Ferry before turning south-west towards Ely. From here the Ely–St Ives branch can be followed to Sutton, then by cutting across to Chatteris the GN&GE joint line can be followed through Somersham and St Ives to Huntingdon thence to Warboys, Ramsey and Holme to see the two branches which never met. If time permits Benwick, close to Ramsey, is worth a visit.

Other possibilities in the Fens are either to stay in Ely, March or Wisbech and then make journeys along the former tracks; alternatively, those proceeding to East Coast resorts could follow east–west routes while journeying to and from the resort.

Particularly rich remains can be found by coming off the A1 at Holme and then following the two Ramsey branches to Somersham. Ramsey stations have all the features which once characterised the main railway aspects of the East Anglian market town, complete with goods sheds, weigh-bridge and sidings on the edge of the towns. Somersham, the junction on the GN&GE, has one of the more complete stations in the Fens, awnings, lamps, platforms and out-buldings are still extant.

By cutting across to Earith, a mere two miles, the Ely–St Ives line can be followed thence to Ely, replete with a number of station houses and crossing-keepers' cottages at Haddenham and Wilburton, dating back to the 1860s. Continuing northwards towards King's Lynn, one enters the territory described in Arthur Randell's *Fenland Railwayman* and his other books. One of his former stations, Magdalen Road, junction for Wisbech, has happily been reopened recently. From here the line to Wisbech, with station remains dating from the 1840s, can be walked. Norfolk's only oilfield, served by the narrow-gauge railway to Setchey, can be visited. Remains of the railway are practically nil but the spoil heaps indicate the terminus of this hopeful inter-war venture.

CHAPTER 5

East Suffolk

East Suffolk is a countryside of sandy hills, marshy valleys with more fertile areas between, leading down to a low cliff-lined coast interspersed with muddy inlets fed by slow-moving rivers. These form the natural harbours of Yarmouth, Southwold, Aldeburgh, Woodbridge, and the Stour and Orwell ports. The original main line across this countryside from Ipswich to Yarmouth was an inland line, built against the grain of the country, to this day remaining a switchback line on the portion still open from Ipswich to Beccles. The line was originally built by the East Suffolk Railway under its initial title of the Halesworth, Beccles & Haddiscoe Railway, opening to passenger traffic on 4 December 1854 as the East Suffolk Railway, and operated by the Eastern Counties Railway. Its original focus was a link with the Norwich to Lowestoft line, connecting it directly with Great Yarmouth and Norwich, reaching the former via the long-defunct Reedham east curve. No sooner was the original plan nearing completion than a southward extension towards Ipswich was sought and approval obtained from Parliament, the Eastern Union Railway planning to meet it half-way, at Woodbridge. Branch lines to Framlingham, Leiston and a goods-only line to Snape Maltings were planned, thus serving an area until then neglected by railways. The main promoters were Sir Samuel Peto, the builder of Lowestoft Harbour and a major railway contractor, and the Ipswich brewer and banker Cobbold, a director of the Eastern Union Railway. Their plan seems to have been for a line from Yarmouth to the

69

Thames, a junction with the London Tilbury & Southend Railway at Pitsea providing access to London completely independent from the Eastern Counties Railway. Such schemes and quarrels over traffic scarcely large enough for one major main line and its branches was typical of this era, and as usual financial problems intervened. Only the nominally-independent links to Yarmouth from Haddiscoe and to Lowestoft from Beccles were built together with the branches to Leiston, Snape and Framlingham, grander ideas being abandoned.

Southwold did not get a service in the original plans, but Bungay was later connected to Beccles by the Waveney Valley Railway. Vigorous competition to the new line came both from river navigations and from coastal schooners. Most of the mills and maltings, warehouses and the few existing factories were built beside the water; few new economic enterprises were started in the early years of the railways in East Suffolk, apart from printing at Beccles and expansion of the agricultural engineering works at Leiston. The railways offered speed, a commodity not in great demand in Victorian East Suffolk. Ships were cheap and Suffolk folk conservative. It was fortunate for the shareholders in this ambitious railway that the Great Eastern Railway was formed a mere three years after opening, enabling them to dispose of their holdings for more firmly-based stocks and thus avoid the perils of bankruptcy. The provision of a second main line into both Yarmouth and Lowestoft allowed for expansion in their traffic; both at that time were approached only by single lines from Norwich. Yarmouth developed as a seaside resort, and both it and Lowestoft increased their fishing fleets and fish trade with London, but since the East Suffolk line and its branches was directed at London none of the lucrative coal hauls were available. Thus a main line was expensively built a mere dozen miles from a parallel line whose connections served the same main places. The rest of the traffic was mainly rural, with a tendency to decline while the

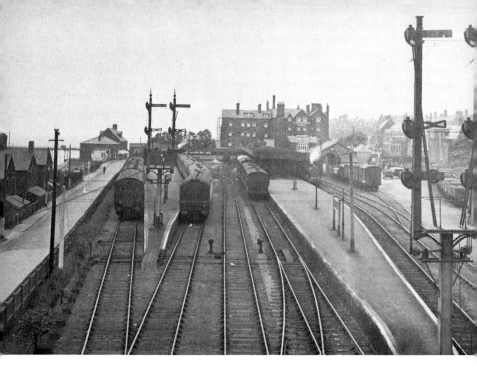

Plates 13 and 14. Two views of Hunstanton Station in June 1931 which today is the site of a fun fair and coach park. The view above looking towards the buffers is interesting for it shows the Eastern Belle Pullman train, a short-lived venture into Pullman services in the GE area. *(L&GRP)*

Plates 15 and 16. Homes by the railway. *Above:* Guestwick station and signal box refurbished and used as house, 1973. *Below:* Crossing-keeper's cottage of concrete blocks, near Themelthorpe, M&GN Melton Constable–Norwich line. Typical of later Marriott design. *(R. S. Joby)*

holiday traffic, though growing, was very seasonal and required extensive facilities which remained idle for much of the year. The line from Ipswich to Lowestoft remains open, together with the goods spur from Saxmundham to a siding beyond Leiston, where heavy goods for Sizewell nuclear power station are dealt with. Attempts have been made to close it throughout, and only strong resistance from local activists led by Mr Gerard Fiennes has prevented this from happening.

The section from Beccles to Yarmouth closed on 2 November 1959, apart from short stretches from Haddiscoe to Aldeby finally closed after the 1964–5 sugar-beet campaign, and the first few hundred yards outside Yarmouth South Town, used briefly as a temporary siding. The chief feature of the line was a pair of swing bridges, the first at Beccles and the second between Haddiscoe and St Olave's. Both were crossed at walking pace and until 1927 required pilotmen on the footplate for the crossing as well as a signalbox and constant maintenance. The cost of keeping this line up to express standards for a short intense flow of traffic in the summer proved prohibitive, especially when the direct line from Yarmouth to Lowestoft was under-used after the closure of the Breydon Viaduct.

For a century the Beccles to Yarmouth line provided for holidaymakers the pleasantest approach to Yarmouth. After a rollercoaster run from Ipswich to Beccles one caught a first glimpse of the Broads on crossing the Beccles Swing Bridge. On a sunny day blue water, teak cruisers and white sails briefly filled the view. The pilotman jumped off as the locomotive cleared the bridge but the train did not accelerate until the last carriage was clear. On a busy Saturday in the early 1950s the 'Easterling' consisted of eight coaches after the Lowestoft portion had been detached at Beccles, so this took several minutes. The B17 Sandringham hauling the train then positively leapt away up the bank past the little red station at Aldeby and dashed down towards the Waveney

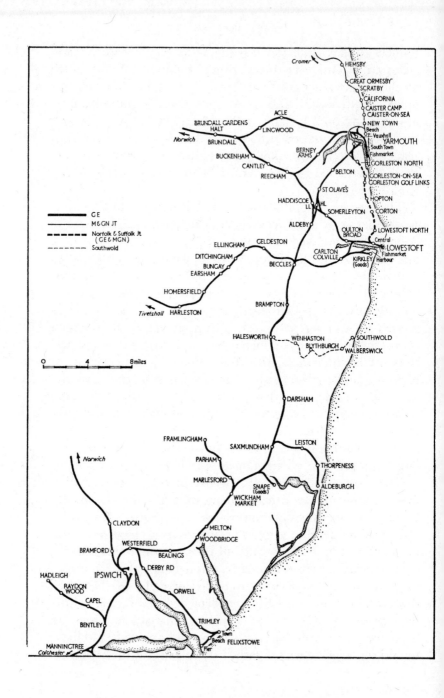

again at Haddiscoe. The marshes are very broad at this point and the view right across to Breydon was not to be missed. On approaching Fleet Junction where the original line to Haddiscoe curved northwards to join the Reedham line at the Low Level station, the main line climbed up to the High Level station, a rather severe concrete and brick building, and then crossed the Waveney on the 1926 St Olave's Swing Bridge, which afforded a fine view of both the river and the New Cut to the north-west. The New Cut was another Peto speculation, designed to make Norwich a sea-going port with an outlet at Lowestoft, which he was developing in the early nineteenth century. Silting defeated the main object of the exercise, but pleasure craft have used the waterway extensively in this century. To the north of the line the vast shimmering expanse of Breydon Water could be seen from time to time, with the old Roman castle at Burgh standing sentinel against the Saxon invader. Yachts distantly viewed appeared as if they were sailing across reed beds and fields. Finally the M&GN line to the Beach station crossed over the line, and the Breydon Viaduct was glimpsed as the train slid into the most commodious of the three Yarmouth stations. One alighted amid a jostling crowd into a busy forecourt where the boys of the town vied with each other to take one's case to the boarding house for a 'tanner'. Dripping boxes of fish littering the platforms gave one a foretaste and smell of many meals to come, while views of the Broads had whetted one's appetite for the steamer cruises available from the Haven Bridge, a few yards from South Town station. This was always a far better introduction to Yarmouth than the broken-down bridge and narrow streets from Vauxhall, or the endless rows of terraced houses around Beach station, which looked just like the Midlands towns from which so many of the visitors were trying to escape.

From 1959 express trains from London to Yarmouth travelled via Lowestoft where they reversed and then ran along the coast line of the old Norfolk & Suffolk Joint to

Yarmouth South Town. This obviated the division of trains at Beccles and gave Gorleston holidaymakers direct access to London, as well as serving the numerous caravan parks and holiday camps at Corton and Hopton. This line was the third route between Yarmouth and Lowestoft to be used. Originally, trains had gone from Lowestoft via Somerleyton then Reedham East Curve, now removed, and into Yarmouth Vauxhall via Berney Arms. The building of the Beccles to Yarmouth line enabled passengers to change from the Lowestoft to Norwich line at Haddiscoe and catch another train at Haddiscoe High Level onwards to Yarmouth. In 1872 this was further improved by the building of the east curve at Haddiscoe, enabling through trains to go direct from Lowestoft to Yarmouth South Town, but the route was only a little less circuitous than the original route. In 1903, after the M&GN and the GER had sunk their differences, a joint line was built to link the two via Hopton and Corton with the additional hope of developing holiday resorts all the way along the coast. A link from Yarmouth Beach to Gorleston North spanned Breydon Water with the magnificent and impressive Breydon Viaduct. The line was double-tracked, the stations modern and convenient, but intermediate traffic stubbornly refused to develop before World War I and some of the little that was generated was lost to the buses after the war. In addition, the Haddiscoe route lost much of its traffic, so that the east curve was closed in 1934 and lifted early in 1939.

Typical local trains between Yarmouth and Lowestoft or either and Beccles consisted of two coaches hauled by a small tank engine, in early days often the M&GN 4-4-2Ts which were constructed for this service. A variety of GER, GNR, and GCR small tanks was used after the grouping, providing a frequent but poorly-patronised motor-train service. Expresses were mainly from the M&GN via the Beach station and Breydon Viaduct. Yarmouth received about five times as many M&GN passengers as Lowestoft, so trains had rather an empty appearance even in mid-summer. Fish was the other major traffic over this line; three or even more specials a day left Lowestoft until the 1920s. The herring season in the autumn was especially busy, when there were also a large number of specials for the Scottish fisher lassies and crewmen. In the 1930s fish traffic fell and holiday developments only partly replaced lost revenue. In 1953, when major repairs to the Breydon Viaduct were required, it was decided that Lowestoft could be adequately served in summer by diverted trains via Norwich Thorpe, so the service from Yarmouth Beach to Lowestoft was abandoned. Traffic increased briefly again in 1959 after the diversion of trains mentioned above but some Yarmouth to London services were diverted to Vauxhall station and routed via Norwich in 1962, this despite the upgrading of the line to take express traffic. Four years later the intermediate stations were made into unstaffed halts, the line singled and a seedy paytrain ran between weedy stations, some of which had been vandalised. Finally, with no prospect of expansion in traffic and a bus service which was adequate for most of the year, the decision was taken and the line closed on 4 May 1970.

Only one railway in East Suffolk never came under the rule of the Great Eastern and that was the splendidly eccentric Southwold Railway, running from Halesworth on the East Suffolk line to the small fishing and trading port and resort of Southwold at the mouth of the river Blyth, a navigable stream which meandered across the marshes from west of Halesworth to become a tidal estuary in its lowest reaches. Southwold had requested that a main-line branch be built, but in the absence of that a tramway was proposed in 1870 under the same Act as the successful Wisbech & Upwell Tramway; as with so many other East Anglian schemes, lack of funds prevented any development of this idea. Eventually at public meetings in Halesworth and Southwold in October 1875, local landowners with support from a narrow-gauge engineer and Richard Rapier of the famous Ipswich engineering firm, who had built narrow-gauge locomotives for export to China, convinced the locals of the need for and low cost of building a narrow-gauge railway. The reporting civil engineer, Arthur Pain, became one of the engineers of the line. The Act for the Southwold Railway Company was passed the following July but delays and resignations of local landowners slowed down progress so that not until 24 September 1879 was the line opened. It was a lightly-engineered line apart from the swing bridge across the Blyth at Southwold. The 3ft 0in gauge made it incompatible with the main line but traffic was never very heavy, while the low cost enabled completion with far less trouble than with so many other lines chronicled. The speed limit of 16mph enforced by the Board of Trade was only a handicap when buses started to compete. Before that it merely meant that the journey over the eight miles took ten minutes longer than over many a typical East Anglian branch line. The local paper described the stations as 'a happy combination of cheapness and convenience and . . . a model of what good architectural taste can do with very circumscribed materials'. The little six-wheeled coaches had open-ended balconies and longitudinal tramway-type seats inside, and were said to be airy and spacious. The loco-motives originally delivered were three 2–4–0 tanks from Sharp Stewart of Manchester, but so strained were company finances that one of these had to be returned to the makers in 1883, while the remaining two were leased back to the railway for £150 a year, although funds were adequate for purchase by 1890. A new third locomotive was purchased three years later, this time a 2–4–2T which apparently ran more smoothly than the first delivered. A dozen four-wheeled wagons sufficed for goods traffic at first, but later a pair of luggage vans appeared in 1885 and three more trucks in 1892. The main East Anglian coal merchant Thomas Moy Ltd also eventually ran sixteen six-wheeled coal trucks on the Southwold Railway.

The sight which greeted main-line passengers at Hales-worth in the years immediately before World War I was unique in East Anglia. A tiny blue locomotive, immaculate paintwork and burnished brass, stood bunker-first at the head of a mixed train of goods wagons, vans, and a couple of maroon coaches. Goods transferred from the main line were heaved bodily across a transshipment platform at the rear of the Southwold Railway station. Passengers from the GER trains crossed by footbridge onto the island platform to join the little train. After running parallel with the main line for a few hundred yards, crossing the main road by separate bridges, the Southwold train swung eastwards through woods and fields, under the road bridge at Holton (which still exists), over the Blyth at Wenhaston Mill and across the sole level-crossing on the line before drawing into Wenhaston station, delightfully rustic apart from its corru-gated iron roof. The Blyth valley widens from here onwards to the sea and broad vistas of water and marsh came closer as Blythburgh was approached. The church on the hill dominated the local scene and the railway respected this eminence by skirting around it in a wide loop, avoiding earthworks and gradients. Blythburgh station was a passing loop, tokens were exchanged here, goods wagons were frequently shunted into the sidings. The train then passed under the only other road bridge on the line, now part of the A12 embankment, and emerged to give a fine view of the ever-widening estuary. Sandy heath and hills now dominated the scene south of the river, the diminutive loco-motive working as hard as possible; despite the low speed it always seemed much faster, as the train was so much nearer the rails than a standard-gauge train. Walberswick was a brief halt, a small isolated station, even after its 1902 enlargement, almost out of view of human habitation at the approaches to the great swing bridge into Southwold. This had been renewed in 1907 at great cost as part of a programme aimed at widening and strengthening the line sufficiently to allow conversion to standard gauge. A long-planned harbour branch was also built just before World War I and included a weighbridge with a few yards of standard gauge line on it. Southwold station with its locomotive and carriage sheds, toilets, bookstall and electric lighting was the most elaborate on the line. With its long, tree-shaded platform piled with luggage, produce baskets and hampers it was the miniature epitome of the Edwardian station in its heyday. The railway company even managed a 2 per cent dividend between 1911 and 1913, only a point behind the GER at its best!

New hopes for traffic were raised when the harbour branch was built in 1914; a new, more powerful o–6–2 tank engine was delivered a month before war broke out. Named *Wenhaston*, this sturdy little Manning Wardle tank did sterling duty alongside *Southwold, Halesworth* and *Blyth*, its tiny companions. The latter two were thirty-five years old in 1914, and together with the rolling stock beginning to show their age. Other plans for extensions to Kessingland, and also for a link from Haleworth to the Mid-Suffolk Light Railway had failed, while the one branch that was built came too late for the rebirth of the Southwold Railway, and of Southwold as a fishing town.

The post-war period was one of continued good traffic but with higher costs and an income which was adequate for modest maintenance but not for renewals or expansion. Wage cuts for the staff and a coat of paint on the platform side only for the carriages helped keep the account books in the black apart from the General Strike year of 1926 when a £4 deficit was recorded, thanks to a large drop in passenger traffic, subsequently recovered. Southwold Corporation allowed passengers to be picked up by buses within its boundaries in 1928, so that there was direct competition for the first time. The railway replied by drastically lowering its fares, lost passengers in addition and just did not have the financial resources to continue a prolonged battle, despite further cuts in wages and promised protection under the Road Transport Bill. The end came on 11 April 1929.

The Southwold Railway was fondly regarded for its idiosyncracies by a host of local and distant admirers. Few transport systems can be recalled with such clarity by so many local people forty-five years after their closure, or be still celebrated by treasured cartoons lovingly shown the visitor so long after their subject has disappeared. The finale of the Southwold Railway was given 'the works' by the media of the day, newsreel, press and journals, with hundreds of people to see the last train which was grossly overcrowded in consequence. Last trains were indeed rarities in those days, even more so were lines closed to goods traffic simultaneously. Many must have been drawn to the wake by the cartoon series the 'Sorrows of Southwold' by Reg Carter, who also did the end-papers of the *Wonder Book of Railways,* the introduction to railway enthusiasm for thousands of boys in the inter-war period. He exaggerated the minor mishaps, the cows on the line, the stops for flower-picking by the lineside, into one of the truly great comic series of the cartoonist. The locomotives and stock in the drawings are identifiable, as are the staff depicted, but purists will bristle at the sight of four-wheeled carriages and locomotives with cylinders under the coal bunker! He was not malicious towards the little railway, and probably helped clients be forbearing when troubles struck. Both sets of cartoon postcards can still be obtained at 'The Venture' in Southwold, a tribute to the power of nostalgia fuelled by a unique little enterprise.

Most of the track can be followed on foot today, the roughest going being at the Halesworth end, so that a start at Holton Bridge is to be advised. Springtime is best for track walking here. Since much of the line was across heath it is relatively dry and vegetation has not started to obstruct progress. The Blyth estuary is spanned by a Bailey bridge where the old swing bridge once operated, so there are no real complications in recreating one of the pleasantest routes in East Anglia. One of the saddest features is that the station at Southwold which stood for nearly four decades after closure has now been replaced by an architecturally un-inspiring fire-station.

In similar countryside, leading to a similar port lay the Aldeburgh branch of the East Suffolk Railway. This is now abandoned from just east of Leiston, the open section being used to service the gigantic Sizewell nuclear power station. Also abandoned was the system linking the branch to the works of Richard Garrett Ltd in Leiston, a firm noted for its variety of farm and road transport vehicles and in later years for its locomotive parts used on Beyer Peacock loco-motives all over the world. Until the late 1950s Garretts used an Aveling & Porter geared compound shunter named *Sirapite* which owed more to a traction engine for its design than to a normal railway locomotive. The large guarded flywheel and the cylinders mounted above the boiler indicated its design origins and its slow (5·6mph maximum speed) chuntering progress differentiated it strongly from anything else seen at Leiston. Originally this tiny locomotive was built for the Mountfield Gypsum Mine Tramway in Sussex on the Charing Cross to Hastings line. Its attraction to Garretts was its small size, low appetite for coal and the fact that its gearing enabled it to handle trucks on a 1 in 38 gradient in the works. Its shining green paint and highly-polished brasswork was a tonic for eyes starved both of colour and brass on post-war country branch lines.

The rest of the branch to Aldeburgh also had its curiosities, not least Thorpeness. The station here was the twenty-first resort station to be opened by the GER, but only a few days before World War I broke out. The resort had been publicised by Peter Pan's creator, Barrie, and like so many others in East Anglia seemed to have a promising future. Provision at first was very modest, with three old railway carriages adapted for the usual station functions, and so it

remained until closure on 12 September 1966. Other attempts
to foster traffic on the Aldeburgh branch included visits of
the 'Eastern Belle' a train of Pullman cars which ran from
Liverpool Street to selected resorts giving a cheap luxury
service to those not able to afford either the time or money
for a longer holiday. Smartly turned-out Cloud Hamilton
4-4-0s enabled the train to get quickly to its destination
in $2\frac{1}{4}$ hours from Liverpool Street, faster than any normal
service, without embarrassing weight restrictions on some
of the lines traversed.

One branch of the ESR never carried regular passenger
traffic, and that was the short line from Snape Junction to
the Maltings at Snape, more famous today for the annual
Aldeburgh Festival which has replaced barley as the chief
attraction of that little port on the River Alde. The impressive
brick maltings were approached through a massive archway
which framed rural industry and its attendant railway in an
architecturally splendid manner. Although it was originally
intended that Snape Junction should have its own railway
station for passengers, only a signal box emerged from the
original plans and the little branch of only a mile-and-a-half
became a mere diversion for a daily pick-up goods service
between Ipswich and Saxmundham, headed for much of this
century by a ubiquitous J15 0-6-0. The lonely marshland
of the Alde valley was crossed by three low timber bridges
which framed the elderly locomotive and its trucks beauti-
fully against the light in one of the most artistic poses
available to the railway photographer. The whole works had
a system of rails serving it and a wharf where a crane
transferred goods from barge to rail or road, and vice versa.

At work around the Maltings, but not on the GER line,
were some curious trucks owned by the maltsters, Messrs
Swonnells, fitted with dumb buffers, two-link chain couplings
and which had no axle-boxes, hence the objection to their
venturing into the main railway system! As in so many
East Anglian sidings, horses were used for shunting here.

The daily return trip was sometimes a struggle for the J15 which was now tender-first. The line across the marshes for the first mile was easy enough, but then there was a steep climb up to the junction on the ground above the river, and this was sometimes only gained after much slipping on the greasy rails and even on occasion a return for a further run at the bank.

Framlingham was reached by a branch from Wickham Market opened at the same time as most of the rest of the ESR in 1859. Until the coming of the Mid-Suffolk Light Railway in the early part of this century, Framlingham was the railhead for a very large area of Suffolk and its station was a major grain despatch point. It was also the epitome of an East Anglian branch terminus, with its small one-engine shed where the resident locomotive spent weekday nights, returning to Ipswich after the last train on Saturday for boiler washout. The water tower was the most prominent point in the station yard and was capable of filling two tenders in turn. Coaling was a manual job from a raised platform, and for this reason low-sided tenders were preferred by the yard staff. Goods traffic was heavy enough for the branch to continue until April 1965, but passenger traffic ended thirteen years previously. Apart from a flurry of activity at the beginning and end of term at Framlingham College the normal traffic was among the poorest in the region. There was, however, one very distinguished passenger during goods-only days in 1956, when the Duke of Edinburgh stayed at Marlesford for the night during his East Anglian tour of that year. A highly polished B1 4–6–0, much larger and grander than anything seen for years, hauled the Royal Train on the branch, another awaiting it at Wickham Market Junction to take the train forward to Lowestoft. Claud Hamilton 4–4–0s were the only other express locomotives regularly to use the Framlingham branch on seaside excursions which were run from most market towns once or twice a year; in this case Felixstowe was the most popular destination. The track followed a delightful tributary of the Alde for most of its course. Today the road is close enough for most of the route and the major remains to be seen from a car without many long detours.

Thus only the main line and a goods spur remain today between Westerfield and Beccles. The byways were each unique in their own way, and their environment is less changed than in many places, so it is very easy to recall the atmosphere of many of these lines by visits today.

CHAPTER 6

Mid-Suffolk

Inland from the coast, Suffolk is mostly a county of boulder clay plateau but with a large area of sandy heath, the Breckland, in the north-west of the county and smaller scattered heaths elsewhere. The two branches which left the Great Eastern Railway at Bury St Edmunds crossed these contrasting landscapes; the line to Thetford cut across the Breckland, while that to Long Melford climbed on to the plateau and snaked its way through much richer arable country. To the east, the much later Mid-Suffolk Light Railway left the Great Eastern main line to Norwich at Haughley, and ended inconclusively beyond Laxfield amid rich arable land.

All three lines were at one time part of much greater strategies, and hopes were expressed that they would form part of through routes, thereby gaining much traffic in addition to the traffic generated by the towns and villages they actually served. The two branches from Bury St Edmunds were seen as the key part of a fourth north–south line from Norfolk to Essex, but shortly after the opening of the Bury–Thetford line, the Bill to amalgamate the lines from Swaffham to Marks Tey was thrown out, and hopes of glory faded. The Mid-Suffolk Light Railway hoped to link with the Southwold Railway, and with this converted to standard gauge would then be able to offer an east–west route terminating in a developing port which it was hoped would rival Lowestoft. These dreams of directors of rural railways were more often dashed than realised. The traffic potential of East Anglia was rarely adequate for more than a single route between even major centres, but the confident provincial Victorian brewer, grocer or country gentleman on the board of a minor railway constantly tried to prove this wrong, and by parleying with outside railway companies, was hopeful of offers for his usually ailing investment.

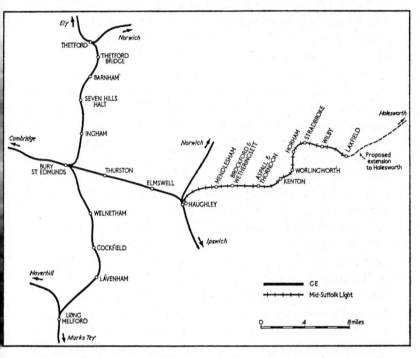

The population of this area is spread unevenly. Bury St Edmunds has been the market and industrial centre for centuries, with Ipswich becoming increasingly important as better transport has allowed its hinterland to grow. South of Bury St Edmunds the textile industries were important in the nineteenth century, towns and villages being often much larger than their counterparts in the rest of Suffolk. Most villages were much more self-contained than they are today, with a large range of crafts and shops in villages where today a general store and garage are often all that is available.

The line from Bury St Edmunds to Thetford was incorporated in 1865, at a time when the Great Eastern was in severe financial trouble, and in no mood to build rural branches of dubious profitability unless threatened by outside competition. Backed by the Member of Parliament, Edward Greene of brewery fame, and the most important local manufacturers and gentry, the line should have had a good start, but the original contractors were sacked, and the new contracts were let a little at a time and were 'prosecuted with the greatest economy'. The line was finally opened eleven years after incorporation with a speed limit of 30mph and a weight limit of 40 tons on locomotives, more suggestive of a light railway than of a link in a prospective main line. The country through which the line ran is still amongst the least inhabited in Suffolk. At the time of opening the total population of the parishes between Bury and Thetford was under 1,000, although the termini were both substantial towns, the former with a population of 13,218 in 1861 and the latter with 4,208 inhabitants. Both were already served by the Great Eastern, so that the main hope of traffic lay with through connections. Officially the Bury St Edmunds & Thetford Railway terminated at Thetford Bridge, whence a spur to Thetford East Junction led via Great Eastern metals to the Thetford & Swaffham Railway. Continued financial problems persisted and calls on shares were not met so that only two years after commencing operations the Great Eastern bought the Bury & Thetford, ended through services north of Thetford and condemned this line to a very quiet rural life.

The initial poverty of the line was reflected in the light engineering, poor stations and reliance on the Great Eastern for stock, locomotives and termini. A service of four return trips a day weekdays only for passengers and one for freight sufficed for most of the life of this line. At both Bury St Edmunds and Thetford there were only two platforms for passengers so that a typical connection would be to arrive

Plates *17 and 18*. Scenes at Snape. *Above:* Class J15 0–6–0 No 65433 crosses the bridge at Snape Maltings. *Below:* Snape Maltings today. *(Dr I. C. Allen)*

Plates *19 and 20.* Station styles – 1. *Above:* Middle Drove, on the King's Lynn–Wisbech line, in 1961. *Below:* Wolferton, then the station for the Royal estates at Sandringham, with Claud Hamilton 4–4–0 No 62539. *(J. Watling, Dr I. C. Allen)*

at Bury St Edmunds from Cambridge, wait on the platform
while the main line train departed. Meanwhile the two-coach
branch train headed by a 2–4–2T simmered on the parallel
track alongside, pulling forward when the line was clear,
then backing-down to pick up passengers, parcels or an
occasional van, and away a few minutes later. Passengers
were generally few, except in wartime. Returning shoppers
from Bury St Edmunds to the villages and Thetford, and
schoolchildren formed the majority of travellers in later
years. Intermediate fares were collected by the conductor-
guard. The line proceeded across heathy sheepwalks through
shallow cuttings and low embankments to the summit at Seven
Hills Halt and thence gently downhill to Thetford Bridge,
past the abandoned spur towards Thetford East Junction and
into the down platform at Thetford. Connections to Ely,
Swaffham and Norwich were usually available within half
an hour. Normal freight traffic was very light, as was the
soil the line traversed. Sheep and rabbit skins were usual
traffic in the early days while timber became important from
the late 1930s. Farm crop traffic was at a much lower level than
on lines to the east and south. The wars however brought
the armed forces and their stores to these deserted heaths
and consequently greatly improved traffic flows. Barnham
Camp in both wars and Honington airfield in World War
II accounted for much of the increased passenger traffic while
the ICI factory and the bomb dump at Barnham generated
three or four extra freight trains daily in World War II. This
traffic continued for nearly fifteen years after the war, when
Barnham became the dump for nuclear bombs as well. The
decline of military traffic and lack of new industry after the
war led to the final decline of this line and its closure to
passengers in 1953 and all traffic in 1960, before the recent
growth of both termini as a result of London overspill.

The Bury St Edmunds–Long Melford branch ran through
much richer country than the Thetford line. Planned by the
Eastern Counties Railway, it was finally built and opened

by the Great Eastern Railway in 1865, linking the Marks Tey–Cambridge line with Bury St Edmunds. Leaving Bury St Edmunds ornate twin-towered station the line turned abruptly southwards, ascended the upper Lark valley to its first station (after the 1909 closure of Bury East Gate) Welnetham, and then ran across the cornfields to the former market town of Lavenham and down into the Stour valley at the aptly-named Long Melford. Like the Thetford line it was single throughout except for passing loops. The population along the route was much greater than that along the Thetford line. Welnetham and Cockfield both served several nearby villages each around its own green and each drew on a population of over 1,000. Lavenham was a small textile town with a generally declining population. It had lost its market seventy years before the railway arrived but still retained occasional country fairs. Long Melford's population grew from 2,870 when the line opened to 3,253 in 1901 but declined to 2,635 by 1921, but was always more substantial than Lavenham's in the railway era. Silk, straw plait, horsehair, coconut and even worsted spinning were the main textile industries of the Stour valley and nearby. They were the remnants of the wool and silk industries which had paid for the magnificent churches of the area. The industries went into steep decline after World War I, as did the population in many towns and villages of this area and traffic on the line.

Train services were usually heavier to Long Melford than to Thetford. Five or six trains a day each way from Bury St Edmunds to Long Melford, with two or three of these continuing to Marks Tey or Colchester sufficed, but in later years this was reduced to four daily. Except for special workings all trains stopped at all stations, and thus provided no real alternative to the Bury–Colchester service via Ipswich. Elderly rolling stock finished its life on this and other lines, which may have added to its charms for the enthusiast but did not help in competition with the parallel road traffic.

The locomotives used included the J15 class with a tender cab for working in reverse. This light 0–6–0 freight locomotive was built from 1883 until 1913 and with various modifications such as dual, vacuum, or Westinghouse brakes and steam heating for passenger work, eventually comprised nearly a third of the Great Eastern locomotive stock. Its universal route availability was of great value on rural branches as was the capacity to tackle anything from a pickup freight to emergency diversions of passenger expresses. The class lasted until the end of steam on the former GER lines and No 65462, the last survivor, can now be seen at Sheringham. Other locomotives which worked the line included the larger J17 class, the E4 mixed-traffic 2–4–0 tender locomotive, and ex-GER tank locomotives.

Today, the track of both the Bury branches has been lifted entirely, but both lines can be easily followed from start to finish with occasional breaks where farming has reclaimed trackbed at the same level as the flanking fields. The Bury-Thetford line stations are now put to various uses. Barnham station is now part of a factory making large metal waste-containers for lorries, while Ingham station is now the centre of a construction company's yard. Seven Hills Halt, a bare platform made of wood, has largely disappeared. The station at Thetford Bridge was a Youth Hostel until 1971, but along with the last mile of trackbed into Thetford, is being redeveloped as part of a road works and London overspill scheme. The station buildings remaining give a good idea of the use of the local black flint in the mid-nineteenth century; simple but durable. Bridge abutments remain and at Ingham station the road bridge over the railway is still complete.

The Bury–Long Melford line operated in rather hillier countryside and consequently there are many more cuttings and embankments with over- and under-bridges across the much denser road network. A particularly good under-line bridge made of local brick reinforced with engineers' blue bricks, can be studied just north of Welnetham station. The intermediate stations are all surviving, Welnetham and Lavenham as private houses and Cockfield as a ruin. The first two stations mentioned are solid structures of local brick and slate-roofed, unusual roofing material in an area known for its tiles and thatch. Cockfield's station buildings were incapable of house conversion, being much smaller and glass-fronted. A cast-iron urinal on the platform also remains, though like the rest of the station sadly vandalised. The station yards have all been used for new purposes, at Lavenham a new factory, a waste pulveriser at Welnetham and a coalyard at Cockfield.

The scenic contrast of the two lines as well as the great amount of remaining material of railway interest makes a run from Thetford to Long Melford well worthwhile. One travels from bleak heathland with twisted pines dotting the horizon, through Bury St Edmunds replete with medieval and eighteenth-century houses, nineteenth-century maltings, and station hotel, and on to some of the most delightful 'green' villages in Suffolk, as well as Lavenham, a veritable treasure house of domestic architecture. Churches of the usual East Anglian richness are of course in all villages.

The 1896 Light Railway Act produced a flurry of plans for light railways throughout rural England, and East Anglia had its quota, mostly built by the GER. Only one private light railway was built eventually, the Mid-Suffolk, and this went bankrupt when only half completed. Until motor lorries became widespread after World War I, local transport in rural areas was by horse-and-cart which was slow and expensive and for many products was prohibitive if the railway station to take the goods to market was more than four or five miles away. Hence if a 'farmer's line' could be built cheaply in areas without railways then it would bring great economic advantages to the community in the form of cheaper coal, fertilisers, seeds and building materials coming in, while making the local farmers as competitive as those elsewhere and allowing the possibility of diversifying into perishable crops as well as ensuring that livestock arrived at market in better condition than they would have after a long drive on the hoof.

Mid-Suffolk is singularly devoid of large market towns, but large villages or decayed market towns with many urban functions form a substitute. The list of trades and facilities available in Laxfield or Stradbroke in 1925 indicated that few of the inhabitants would need to travel for their wants very often. Just under thirty trades, shops and services were available in each village although the population was declining. The plan was to join as many of these large villages as possible between Haughley Junction and Halesworth, with a branch southwards from Kenton to Westerfield, near Ipswich. These plans were approved in 1901 when a Light Railway Order sanctioning forty-two miles of track was published. Permission was granted to raise £300,000 in debentures and preference shares, thus hoping to build the line at the low figure of £7,142 per mile including legal costs, land and buildings. A year later the first sod was cut by the Duke of Cambridge at Westerfield at a ceremony attended by over six hundred guests. Seemingly the renaissance of rural England was about to begin and for the next two years building progressed slowly, but by the middle of 1904 most of the capital had been spent, Halesworth was unapproachable by the original route owing to marshy ground, and East Suffolk County Council refused a loan of £25,000 to compete the lines. Revenue at last started to come in when goods traffic commenced from Haughley to Laxfield in September 1904. Passenger traffic was not to be introduced until the completion of the line, but seven old Metropolitan District Railway carriages were bought cheaply when that system was electrified and disposed of its surplus stock. The locomotives were ordered in 1903 from Hudswell Clarke and delivered in 1904, 1905 and 1909. They were small o–6–oTs with an axle weight of under 10 tons and since speed was limited to 25mph, wheels of 3ft 4in diameter. Stations were mostly small corrugated iron structures at the intermediate stations, while at Haughley and Laxfield the buildings were clad with zinc-coated sheets of iron in a brickwork pattern, which was then painted to look like brick buildings. Remnants can still be seen in Laxfield station, now much weathered.

Disputes with the contractors and the bankruptcy of the first chairman, Mr Stevenson, who was also the local member of Parliament, and the blocking by the debenture-holders of promised loans from Halesworth Council and the Treasury culminated in the Receiver being called in and all building ceasing. The line was used by freight traffic as far as Cratfield but it was not until 1908 that the existing track was sufficiently improved for passenger services to commence between Haughley and Laxfield. A small surplus of £500 over running expenses was now being made but this was needed to catch up with interest arrears rather than new construction or improvements.

In spite of the problems a passenger alighting at Haughley Junction a few years before World War I would have found a very smart little train awaiting him at the Mid-Suffolk platform. A highly-polished dark brownish-red locomotive resplendent with polished brass dome and other metalwork would be standing at the head of two or more brown four-wheeled coaches, an assortment of open and covered wagons and an elderly passenger brake van of 1880s vintage bought from the GER. The first problem was for the tiny locomotive to storm Haughley bank and take its train up and over the 1 in 42 climb, while turning sharply eastwards. If the loads were heavy or the rails slippery the train might have to be set back for a further attempt.

Starts were always jerky as the loose-coupled wagons behind the passenger coaches were suddenly pulled forward. The train then puffed sedately through the cornfields until Mendelsham came into view when the driver applied the engine and coach brakes while the guard, alerted by the whistle, tightened his brakes as the wagons started to run forward and crash into the buffers of the preceding vehicles. A pony and trap stood at the station to convey travellers and their baggage to surrounding villages and farms. The locomotive did any necessary shunting then set off for Brockford & Wetheringsett, a station so deficient in traffic that its receipts were amalgamated with those of Mendelsham. Fast work was called for at the stations if there were many wagons. The sixty-seven minute schedule for nineteen miles was not easy to keep if the speed limit was strictly adhered to; needless to say it was sometimes breached. Aspall & Thorndon served the large village of Debenham as well, but the original hopes were for a branch through Debenham from the next station, Kenton Junction. This was actually laid to within 150yd of Debenham and probably used for a few months unofficially but this had ceased by the end of 1906. Kenton had two platforms, signals, a locomotive shed and the largest intermediate goods yard. Tokens were exchanged here and the locomotive took on water before continuing northwards through Horham to the large village of Stradbroke. A wagon body and a shed stood on the single low platform, but Stradbroke had a staff of two, including the line's finance clerk. By now the majority of the wagons had been shunted into their terminal sidings, and since there was little intermediate traffic nothing had been added. When the delightful village of Laxfield was reached the passenger coaches went no further but the locomotive always had to go up the line, sometimes with wagons for Laxfield Mill and on to Cratfield until 1912, or otherwise just for water at the rickety tank, filled by an old petrol engine from a nearby pond.

The Mid-Suffolk Light Railway certainly tried to serve its unpromising district well from its limited resources. The returning traveller would see churns of milk and boxes of produce loaded en route, especially soft fruit in season. Loaded cattle trucks were a special feature on Tuesdays, the day of the big Ipswich market. Cheap market tickets were also available on Tuesdays. Sunday passenger trains were run until 1921 with special cheap tickets to encourage custom. Spick-and-span, but run on a shoe-string, the Mid-Suffolk continued to provide a good service until the grouping, but between 1908 and 1921 monthly receipts halved while co-operation with the GER increased.

The railway grouping of 1923 did not initially include the Mid-Suffolk, as it seemed such a certain liability, but it was eventually taken over by the LNER in 1924. An economy drive followed. The individualistic locomotives and stock departed, staff numbers were pruned, and mechanical work was moved to Ipswich. The east–west orientation of the line and the low speeds meant a loss of passengers, most of whom wanted to go direct to Ipswich in the south. Freight traffic as elsewhere succumbed to road transport except for sugar beet, a new crop in the 1920s which was processed at Bury St Edmunds by a factory which encouraged rail delivery.

World War II brought a great increase in traffic with the airfields to be supplied at Mendelsham and Horham, and after the war schoolchildren to Stowmarket Grammar School greatly increased the passenger loads morning and evening. In the years before closure this was probably the line with the cleanest locomotives in England. Ipswich J15s had become the normal ones, stationed at Laxfield during the week with a driver and fireman who lodged there. They took a particular pride in scrupulous cleanliness, getting out at intermediate stations to brush off any ash. Brassware was kept polished, while the inside of the cab was recognisably creamy white. It was a revelation in what pre-war standards had been after the general run of post-war dirt and neglect. A further bonus for the enthusiast was the ease with which goods-brake and footplate rides could be obtained, once Haughley had been safely left behind.

Such an individual line attracted a good deal of attention in its last week in July 1952, but after the event, with freight

98

traffic ended the line was torn up within a year. Haughley station yard retains its outline in front of the seed silo which dominated the last years of the Mid-Suffolk's junction, but the rails have long been lifted. The steep bank away from the station can be followed until bushes bar the way. Further along, a gap in the hedge at Brockford, the pond at Kenton, the low platform at Stradbroke can be discerned by the enquiring eye, but the most evocative remains are at Laxfield where the old platforms now look down on a silage heap; the floorboards of the remaining building have rotted but the structure remains standing. Rail grooves across the many level-crossings have long been tarred over and much of the trackbed has been incorporated in enlarged fields. The distinctive Kenton nameboard is still to be seen in the Railway Museum, York. The only bridge abutments still to be seen are surprisingly on the long-abandoned branch. Just north of Debenham where the line crossed the B1077, abutments 20ft 0in high, made of local brick, face each other across the road. A culvert passes under the adjacent embankment, and the embankments are overgrown with mature deciduous trees. Where the A140 crosses the Haughley–Laxfield line the road surface has been lowered, and the trackbed to the east is now used as a linear scrapyard. Mendelsham is now occupied by a large modern malting factory, while Kenton yard has been used for farmyard extensions. This was the shortest-lived of the trio of lines and has left the smallest imprint on the modern landscape, but its memory lives for all those who travelled on it.

In all the three lines described here it was hoped that the coming of the railway would arrest the decline of the areas served, but this was not to be. Instead the railway provided a new outlet for the locally-produced materials but brought little new industry to the intermediate stations. The remaining population was undoubtedly better served in respect of goods and services from outside and this weakened the old village trades.

CHAPTER 7

Cambridge & District

Cambridge has always been an admirable centre from which to study railways, and a point from which to sally forth to see lines both working and redundant. The station itself, well away from the university sector of the town, is unique with its long single main-line platform and central crossover, bays at either end catering for branch lines and former services to other railways. The GER made Cambridge one of its main junctions, while the LNWR from Bedford and Bletchley, the GNR from Hitchin, and the Midland from Kettering provided a wide variety of colour and locomotive and rolling stock interest. Each line had its own facilities and goods yards wherever possible, adding to the confusion of the mere traveller, but delighting the undergraduate railway enthusiast.

One of the earliest main line abandonments took place in the Cambridge district. Before the GNR main line opened up direct communication to the north George Hudson, the 'Railway King', attempted to create a direct line to York in 1845 incorporating the Northern & Eastern main line being built towards Cambridge from London. From this the Newmarket Railway intended to build a line from Great Chesterford, where the Northern & Eastern was to make a junction, via Newmarket and eventually to join the Norfolk Railway at Thetford, making a through route to Norwich which would avoid both Cambridge and Ely and be considerably shorter than any alternative route. With the title of the Newmarket & Chesterford Railway, a line between these two places was opened on 3 January 1848 to goods and on 4 April to passengers, using its own equipment. By this date, the Railway Mania was collapsing, investors were becoming wary of expansionist schemes likely to cost them money, with returns on that money seeming increasingly unlikely. Yet here was a railway proposing to compete with the Eastern Counties Railway over a shorter route at a time when a third route to Norwich was nearing completion further east. Nemesis in the form of creditors, and the working arrangement with the ECR overtook the Newmarket & Chesterford Railway in October of the year of opening. Services continued erratically until October 1851, but included a three-month suspension of service. Finally, on 9 October 1851, the section from Six Mile Bottom to Newmarket was incorporated into a through line from Cambridge to Bury St Edmunds via Newmarket and the section between Great Chesterford and Six Mile Bottom was closed to all traffic, being dismantled by the Eastern Counties Railway in 1858 after formal take-over. The line was not forgotten, especially by Newmarket racegoers who petitioned for its reopening several times in order to avoid lengthy delays at Cambridge. In 1892 the Duke of York (later King George V) signed a memorial to the Chairman and Directors of the Great Eastern Railway, adding his name to a distinguished list of well-known turf personalities interested in the Newmarket Races, but to no avail. The original purpose was never consummated and Cambridge dominated local traffic; by-passing it was obviously an unforgivable sin. The course of this long-abandoned line is still quite clear as a series of earthworks alongside the A11 near Six Mile Bottom and tree belts to this day, a memento of competition overdone in the Railway Mania, and a reminder of the fate of losers when faced with the might of the big battalions.

Before World War I the small black LNWR locomotives added a fourth colour to the green, blue, and red locomotives at Cambridge, with 'plum-and-spilt-milk' carriages giving

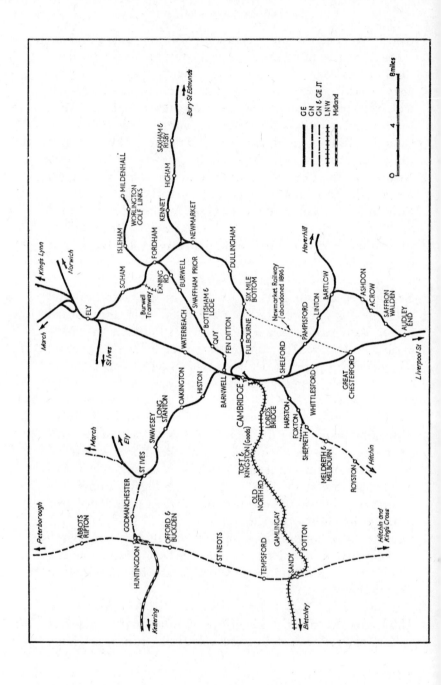

further miscellany to the varnished teak and deep red of the other incumbents. Although they all used the same passenger station each had its own goods station, the GER on the eastern side of the main line, the others arranged *en echelon* with the LNWR just north of its junction with the GER, followed by the GNR just south of the passenger station, while the MR held aloof to the north. Each had its own uniformed staff vying with each other for smart turnout, and often pretending ignorance of the other companies' activities when passengers made enquiries about services of other lines. Yet there was company logic behind these incivilities, especially where the more lucrative goods traffic was concerned. In terms of mileage the most sensible way of delivering general goods or coal from Nottingham to Cambridge was by Midland Railway to Peterborough, then by GER to Cambridge, but after the Railway Clearing House had divided the receipts the LNWR, as the originating company, would have had only a tiny share. Far better from its point of view to ship the goods via its joint line to Market Harborough then via Northampton, Bletchley and thence to Cambridge where unloading could take place in the LNWR goods shed. Agents were sent around factories, warehouses, and farms to entice goods to their own companies, offer discounts, and route goods often as much as twice the distance of the shortest route; their orders always were to get the traffic even if it made economic nonsense. This predilection could be turned to account by passengers who wished to see a lot of the countryside for the minimum cost, as passenger tickets were priced via the shortest route but competing companies offered their tickets at the same price. Cambridge to Swansea via Birmingham and Shrewsbury was a particular bargain for those with stamina or who wished to make a chain of visits en route!

The LNWR route to Cambridge saw several experiments in its long career. The Tyer electric tablet system for working single lines safely had originally been tried out on the

M&GN lines, but this line was the one used for the earliest experiment with a major company in 1887. After the grouping the LMS experimented with several types of diesel railcar on its lines in the South Midlands, and in 1938 the very smart streamlined three-car set with sliding doors was on a regular run between Oxford and Cambridge. Of the pre-war diesels it was the most promising apart from those of the GWR, but World War II prevented further experiment and development. In the same vein, after closure on New Year's Eve 1967 the line has since become the site of a very long radio-telescope belonging to Cambridge University. This is sited between the old Lord's Bridge station and the junction with the GER. The long level and straight stretch was ideal for this futuristic-looking apparatus, being the nearest suitable abandoned line to Cambridge.

A GER branch line from Cambridge which constantly delighted many generations of enthusiasts was that from Cambridge to Mildenhall, opened in two parts, from Cambridge to Fordham Junction on the Ely to Bury St Edmunds line on 2 June 1884 and thence to Mildenhall the following 1 April. Until the recent influx of Londoners, Mildenhall was a small market town on the edge of the Fens, in recent years also acting as a service centre for two large American airbases. The problem with this line was always the thinness of passenger traffic and consequently there was always an interest in new ways of how to run this cheaply. The conventional device of few trains was constant, three return trips being normal, and in the nineteenth century the GER also lowered capital costs by using superannuated locomotives and stock which were not always economical on fuel and repairs. A breakthrough was made in 1913 by starting a push-and-pull train on this line to replace the time-consuming turn-round at Mildenhall, were the small tender locomotives were laboriously turned by hand at the end of each trip. The lightweight 1300 class (later F7) 2-4-2 tank locomotive was used together with a composite car for thirty third-class and nine first-class passengers, together with a driving car for forty-six passengers, a guard's van and driving compartment equipped with compressed air controls fed from the locomotive's Westinghouse pump. Such a set posed many problems, such as lack of capacity on market days when luggage was very heavy, the impossibility of substituting locomotive or carriages if mechanical failures took place, and the extreme difficulty of running mixed trains when traffic was light. The GER reverted to more conventional trains; typically an E4 2–4–0 with a short rake of elderly coaches using a conductor-guard became the rule until diesels took over in 1958.

Whenever war threatened the government made great efforts to maximise home food production, and during World War I the GER was encouraged to run a special egg and poultry train to market towns such as Mildenhall. Local advertising lured the farmers and poultrymen down to the station yard where they were shown new methods, models of the latest equipment, grading was demonstrated, and the participants later fed in a restaurant car attached to the train. Quintupled egg output was hoped for, but not achieved. Such occasions were rare in market towns like Mildenhall, but the GER was a railway which tried very hard to raise farming incomes by demonstrations, and spread the gospel of better methods in all types of farming. The company hoped to reap its own reward later with more traffic, especially the better-paying produce traffic. A van filled with strawberry punnets on their way to Stratford Market, another GER initiative, was worth many truckloads of potatoes.

In the late 1950s British Railways seemed anxious to save as many passenger lines as possible by introducing new railcars and revamping services. By that time a 128-seat two car dmu was overprovision on the Mildenhall run, but a number of Maybach-engined four-wheel railbuses came into service and the Mildenhall and Saffron Walden lines received them. With fifty-four seats, or double that if two were coupled together, these nippy four-wheeled cars gave a brief revitalisation to the lines long inured to the oldest stock and locomotives. They were amusing to watch as they wove away northwards from Cambridge towards Barnwell Junction, lurching over the numerous points in crossing that complicated network of lines. For passengers, however, the inconvenient station at Cambridge whose site was ordained by Victorian dons was used less and less, whereas Drummer Street bus station was next to the shops. Cars were being bought in East Anglia more than elsewhere in the country in relation to the population so that a line such as this which had had thin traffic from the start was an early victim of closure even before the Beeching Report, and so passenger services ceased on 18 June 1962. Goods traffic ceased in two stages, as a result of the Report the final stub from Fordham to Burwell closing on 19 April 1965. As in the case of Haverhill the coming of thousands of Londoners to expand the population and commerce of the town did not stay the execution.

Of the lines that intruded into Cambridge from their own heartlands only the GNR main line from King's Cross remains, and with electrification from King's Cross to Royston the passenger traffic over the remainder of that may well wither later. The Midland Railway entered Cambridge via the Ely & Huntingdon Railway which had an end-on junction at Huntingdon and then joined the line from March at St Ives. Through services were provided to Kettering and as a cross-country line it could be classified as useful at peak times and for minor connections, but hardly vital. Many RAF personnel well remember it as a means of getting from East Anglia to Cardington or vice-versa and it was one of several lines whose passenger traffic declined remarkably as National Service was phased out in the late 1950s.

One of the features of the journey from St Ives westwards was the number of weak timber bridges, and only light locomotives such as the old Midland 2–4–0s of Kirtley, GER

Plates 21 and 22. Station styles – 2. *Above:* The stark simplicity of the Audley End branch platform at Bartlow Junction, with the diesel railbus in use in September 1964. *Below:* GER solidity epitomised in the station buildings at Wretham & Hockham on the Thetford–Swaffham line, in 1963. *(J. Watling)*

Plates 23 and 24. Tram engines. *Above:* No 68217, lettered 'British Railways', working on the Wisbech & Upwell Tramway, south of Wisbech, in 1950. *Below:* Sentinel shunter, LNER No 38, on Lowestoft Quay, in 1947. *(Dr I. C. Allen)*

E4s and J15s as well as the later ubiquitous class 2MT 2–6–0s
were permitted to use the line, and then only single-headed.
The propensity of the bridges to catch fire in dry weather
was a constant trial to the civil engineers and further limited
the usefulness of the line. Platforms at the stations were
short. At St Ives only three coaches could be accommodated
and four at Huntingdon East alongside the GNR main
line station. The usefulness of this as a transfer point for
Cambridge people on to East Coast main line trains was
limited by the lack of expresses stopping there. Few lines
with good cross-country potential could have suffered so
many handicaps to traffic, yet for the railway enthusiast it
was these drawbacks which added the spice of interest—
antique locomotives, one of the prettiest routes in the district
through orchards and water meadows, the line crossing
and recrossing the sluggish Ouse as Godmanchester and
Huntingdon were approached. All this could be taken in at
a leisurely pace, as there was a speed limit of 40mph over
most of the line and 10mph over some bridges, while its
being single track to St Ives further limited its capacity.
Only one long-distance train with express pretensions used
the line, a Birmingham to Clacton summer Saturday service
in the early 1950s, which was no faster over the Huntingdon
to St Ives section than other trains, but ran non-stop thence
to Cambridge.

The other intruder to be seen at Cambridge was the LNWR
whose line eventually went right through to Oxford via
Sandy, Bedford and Bletchley. Part of the route was the
Sandy & Potton Railway, dealt with in another volume in
this series. The section between Potton and Cambridge was
opened on 1 August 1862 as the Bedford & Cambridge
Railway, being operated by the LNWR from the start and
absorbed by it three years later. The basic idea of the East
Coast and the West Coast Main Lines each extending long
arms on either side of their trunk route was taken to
extremes in this case, but for a century it did provide an

invaluable cross-country route far superior to the Cambridge–Kettering route and less prone to congestion than the GER route via Ely and Peterborough. As a link between the two ancient seats of learning it was also frequently patronised both by academics and aspiring students. The morning and evening semi-fast services enabled the round trip to be made in the day, while for many years after World War II there was an afternoon express from Oxford to the more junior university city, which did the journey in just over $2\frac{1}{2}$ hours. There was no reciprocity, as all trains leaving Cambridge in the Oxford direction stopped at every station.

Cambridge is an ideal centre from which to examine the differing practices in construction of several railways when examining their remains. The GER branch to Mildenhall represents late construction by that railway and with well-preserved stations at Barnwell Junction, Fordham and Mildenhall as well as bridges at Barnwell and Wortwell there is much to see. The LNWR line to Oxford has several stations typical of that line. Old North Road has not only the station house but also goods shed and signal box, enabling contrasting architectural styles to be seen close to the city. Potton predates the LNWR in East Anglia, still possessing its Bedford & Cambridge Railway roof brackets. The Newmarket Railway earthworks have already been noted, but the original Newmarket station, although near an open line, is well worth a visit. An ornate building from the late 1840s, it is to be preserved but has yet to be restored. The line from Cambridge to Huntingdon is still largely intact from Cambridge to St Ives, with the prospect of its being re-opened for a limited passenger service. It has many of the features of adjoining lines now closed and is therefore worth a visit, especially to St Ives Junction where the station has been developed under five railway regimes.

Variety has always been the keynote for railways at Cambridge, and along with Peterborough it was the only place in East Anglia where four companies operated to provide that variety. Although much uniformity has been imposed on the Cambridge railway scene it is still well worth a visit, for its unique station alone and makes a very good centre for railway visits in an area which does not permit the linear approach advocated in other chapters.

CHAPTER 8

Essex–Suffolk Borders

It was once possible to travel by rail from Audley End, where the Eastern Counties Railway passed through a gap in the East Anglian Heights, along the borders of Essex and Suffolk to Haverhill, then have a choice of two routes to Marks Tey, and finally reach the North Sea at Brightlingsea. Of this most picturesque route only the main line from Marks Tey to Colchester and Wivenhoe plus the threatened branch from Marks Tey to Sudbury remain. As with so many of the east–west routes in East Anglia the direct routes by road to main centres are much shorter, so railway traffic atrophied and ceased in the 1960s.

The valleys of the Stour and the Colne were the centres of a very busy textile industry which had as one of its Victorian entrepreneurs no less a person than Samuel Courtauld, founder of Britain's largest textile firm. Constable and Gainsborough lived in and painted this countryside making it world famous. The old wool towns and villages are some of the best-preserved and most beautifully-sited in East Anglia with richly architectural flint churches, timber-framed houses and vistas unchanged in places since they were set on canvas by Constable. The railways in this peaceful area were never obtrusive or busy enough to make themselves a nuisance; a railway enthusiast would say that they enhanced the scene. Only the Stour Valley line, part of the through route from Cambridge to Colchester, had any pretentions to being a main line, and even there most of that traffic went via Bury St Edmunds on the double-tracked main line.

The fact that the Cambridge main line took a valley route on its descent from Audley End tunnel meant that Saffron Walden, a large market town in North-East Essex, was missed by the railway. Since the ECR as usual refused to build a branch line, initiative was taken within the town by a local banker and other interested parties, including the Great Eastern Railway after its 1862 incorporation. Although a very short line, the first section from Audley End to Saffron Walden was not opened until 21 November 1865 and yet the much hillier section across to Bartlow was completed eleven months later, giving the Saffron Walden Railway a second junction, this time with the Cambridge to Colchester line. Although the route has been used for traffic diversions when the line south of Cambridge has been blocked, through traffic has never been encouraged and the bulk of the services have been concentrated on the short initial stretch from Audley End to Saffron Walden.

The period when Saffron Walden had its own service to London was in the years after the 1877 purchase of the line by the GER. A through train to London was run until 1894 using a pair of elderly but serviceable Sinclair 2–2–2s, the last in service, which were the only express locomotives light enough to reach Saffron Walden. In 1957, when heavy works at Great Chesterford prevented use of the main line, Britannia Pacifics with full trains moved gingerly along the now reinforced branch, worked by staff-and-ticket. The arrangement was that the express train went forward with the ticket while a light B1 4–6–0 followed with the staff as far as Bartlow where electric tablet working enabled this expensive practice to be dispensed with.

More conventional push-and-pull services on the branch were handled for much of its career by 0–4–4Ts of classes G4 and later G5 which seemed to suit the line better than the more usual GER 2–4–2 wheel arrangement of the feeble F7s. In the 1950s pre-clerestory express stock dating from 1897 was to be seen here long after its demise almost every-

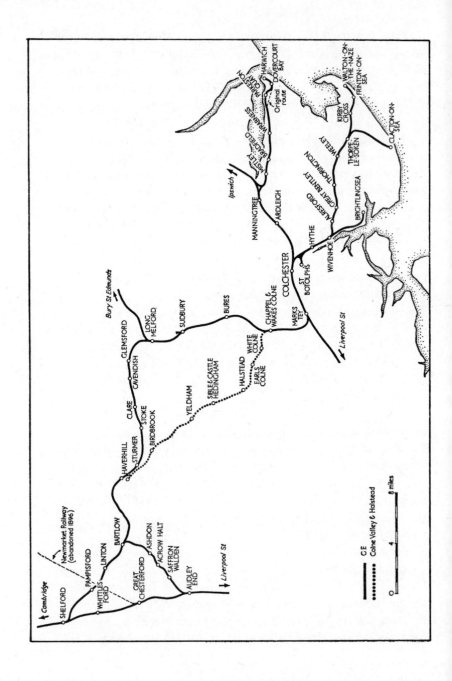

SHELFORD

← Cambridge

PAMPISFORD

LINTON

WHITTLES
FORD

BARTLOW

Newmarket Railway
(abandoned 1896)

GREAT
CHESTERFORD

ASHDON

ACROW HALT

SAFFRON
WALDEN

AUDLEY
END

← Liverpool St

HAVERHILL

STURMER

STOKE

BIRDBROOK

YELDHAM

CLARE

CAVENDISH

GLEMSFORD

LONG
MELFORD

SUDBURY

Bury St Edmunds →

SIBLE & CASTLE
HEDINGHAM

HALSTEAD

EARLS
COLNE

WHITE
COLNE

BURES

CHAPPEL &
WAKES COLNE

MARKS
TEY

COLCHESTER

ST
BOTOLPHS

HYTHE

WIVENHOE

Liverpool St →

ALRESFORD

GREAT BENTLEY

THORRINGTON

WEELEY

BRIGHTLINGSEA

MANNINGTREE

ARDLEIGH

Ipswich →

MISTLEY

BRADFIELD

WRABNESS

PARKESTON QUAY

HARWICH

DOVERCOURT
BAY

Original
route

KIRBY
CROSS

WALTON-ON-
THE-NAZE

FRINTON-ON-
SEA

THORPE
LE-SOKEN

CLACTON-ON-
SEA

GE

Colne Valley & Halstead

0   4   8 miles

where else. The branch train waited at a sharply-curved platform on the eastern side of the station, a pair of dull brown push-and-pull coaches ready to depart. The journey through the woods was best in the autumn; the line was steep and there was a special quality to the exhaust sounds when in woodland, enhanced by the leafy splendour. Later when N7 0–6–2Ts were released from London suburban service these replaced the aged G5s and hauled the first train into the newest station on the line, Acrow Halt, just north of Saffron Walden town itself. The halt was named after the engineering company whose works it served, and the opening was ceremonial with the driver and fireman each being given a bottle of champagne, not of course to be inbibed until that worthy pair went off duty. This event, in March 1957, was a kind of swan-song for the line. A year later a rail-bus was introduced, indicative of the reduced number of passengers. Audley End was busier than ever as a commuter station, often with passengers from Saffron Walden itself who lived a long way from the station and so were driven direct to the main line. After the Beeching Axe was swung at Saffron Walden in September 1964 the Audley End car park at the station was enlarged to cover the old branch line platform—conquest complete.

At Bartlow the cross-country line from Colchester to Cambridge was joined. Typical of the lavish provision of equipment on some lines was the building of two signalboxes at Bartlow as well as at Sudbury, Long Melford and Haverhill. Economy forced the concentration on one box at each place after the LNER took over working in 1923. The line linked a string of textile and market towns of which the most important was Sudbury, yet it was parallel with another east–west line on either side only ten and fifteen miles distant plus the formerly independent Colne Valley Railway between Haverhill and Chappel & Wakes Colne.

Despite such competitive contiguity with other lines the line was built so that it could be doubled if necessary and was upgraded so as to take most of the twentieth-century express passenger locomotives such as Claud Hamiltons, B12s, and Sandringhams. Freight locomotives as large as ex-WD 2–8–0s and J18s made it evident that this was regarded as an alternative to the Cambridge, Bury St Edmunds and Ipswich line, and was so used in wartime. Excursions from or via Cambridge to Clacton also were routed via Sudbury, often headed by unusual locomotives on long-distance passenger trains, for instance a double-headed J15 with an E4, or in later years a class 2MT with whatever else happened to be available. For trains which turned round at intermediate stations tender-first working was often necessary and several of the older tender locomotives were equipped with tender cabs made from materials salvaged from the cabs of scrapped locomotives, much more comfortable than a flapping tarpaulin between the tender and the main cab roof, which was the lot of so many drivers who when driving like this complained of being 'frozen in front and roasted at the rear'.

Connections at Marks Tey in the days of slip coaches were well worth watching. The express would speed through the main line station almost out of sight of the Stour Valley train tucked away on its very sharply-curved platform, then a minute or two later the slip coach with its own guard would glide into Marks Tey as if by magic. After the passengers had alighted the yard locomotive towed the slip coach into a siding to await its return on a London-bound train. The great problem with slip coaches was the impossibility of linking them to moving trains but for many years before World War I they served the useful function on the GER (and especially on the GWR) of giving rural junctions and their connecting branches fast services that they otherwise would not have merited.

Before 1923 another railway ran trains into the branch platform at Marks Tey, and that was the Colne Valley Railway. This was one of the few railways in East Anglia which both remained independent until the grouping and also had its own locomotives and rolling stock throughout until 1923. Often trains of both CVR and GER stock were run to the junction at Chappel & Wakes Colne, where the CVR tank locomotive took over its section of the train in the care of a very smartly-uniformed guard. The locomotive was likely to be a smart black 2–4–2T after the style of the Lancashire & Yorkshire Railway, the carriages were four-wheelers and were painted 'drab' with black-and-yellow lining. In conformity with the GER at either end of the line a Westinghouse brake was used on each of the four locomotives. By the turn of the century the CVR was enjoying its first and last period of prosperity relative though that term was, as it never paid an Ordinary dividend. Although the GER had the right to take over the running of the CVR for half the gross receipts it never did, but helped the smaller company by repairing its rolling stock and locomotives at Stratford, a service it also performed for the Mid-Suffolk Light Railway and the Southwold Railway. Running repairs were undertaken at Haverhill until 1906 when the works was transferred to Halstead, the largest town on the line, where it joined the long-established general office and main locomotive shed. The stables at Halstead were the base of a fleet of half a dozen carts which served the mills and countryside for up to ten miles from Halstead.

The valley along which the polished little train steamed was visibly busy, if not industrialised in the northern sense. After a steep climb up gradients as great as 1 in 60 and a brief stop at the halt-like White Colne the train entered the most substantial station on the line at Earl's Colne (Colne until 1908) which even today hardly looks as if it were built over seventy years ago. Agricultural engineering was the mainstay here, producing a famous turnip chopper so well built as to be useable after many decades. The run alongside the river into Halstead was very picturesque, a mixture of light green grass in the valley bottom and well-tended scattered trees with tilled fields visible to the upward glance.

The metropolis of the valley was and still is Halstead. Courtauld's silk mills, a foundry, flour mills, and tanners made this one of the largest inland settlements in Essex beyond the London fringe. After 1906 over half the staff of the CVR was based here and the goods yard was usually the busiest on the line. A rarity sometimes to be seen was the American rail cycle departing on a rail inspection tour, a change from the hand-pumped truck favoured by most British lines. When traffic was light or a locomotive was unavailable, shunting at Halstead was done by horse, adding a pleasant rural touch to the quietly bustling scene. The signalbox at Halstead was newer than most on the line due to its predecessor being rammed by the Hawthorn Leslie tank engine *Colne* in 1890, one of the few serious accidents on the line.

The remainder of the pleasant journey to Haverhill passed through similar country but with fewer industries, a brickworks at Castle Hedingham and mills and workshops at Haverhill, where most CVR trains used the GER station as connections were usually required with Stour Valley trains. The old CVR station gradually lapsed into a half-life of goods and occasional passenger trains before amalgamation with the LNER in 1923 made it redundant.

Two lines in adjacent valleys each serving only one larger settlement was less than profitable for both. Renewals were more than the private company could afford and even in its period of greatest prosperity it bought redundant Metropolitan Railway carriages in 1905 after the electrification of some of that railway's lines. Civil engineering structures remained light and the one new station of this century was thanks to a loan from the Earl's Colne industrialist. The CVR was a well-loved line in its locality and long after merging into the LNER and even after the greater merger into BR it maintained an individuality both in the appearance of the stations and in the pride the less mobile staff took in keeping stations spick-and-span and florally delightful.

Many of the Stour Valley trains ran through to Colchester on the direct services from Cambridge, typically three coaches plus any vans available made up the train in steam days and the Stour Valley line was one of the few where the ubiquitous J15 0–6–0s could show their paces, sometimes getting up to speeds of over 60mph and not at all inferior in timekeeping to the Intermediate E4 2–4–0s.

Colchester was the junction for the last stretch of line, taking one right down to the coast along the Colne estuary to Brightlingsea through the Tendring Hundred. This peninsula between the Colne and Stour is a pleasant rolling countryside pierced by long muddy creeks. To the north is Harwich, the next-door resort of Dovercourt Bay, and Parkeston Quay, named after GER director Charles Parkes and best known for its continental packet boats. In the mid-nineteenth century the present town of Clacton which dominates the peninsula hardly existed; the long stretch of sands thence to Jaywick barely beginning to be developed. Thus the early promotions in the south of this peninsula aimed at serving the fishing and trading port of Brightling-sea rather than the more speculative investment of building a railway to a potential resort area. The promotion which attempted to do this, the luckless Mistley, Thorpe & Walton Railway had much money spent on it and many earthworks completed between incorporation in 1863 and abandonment in 1869, yet there was a competing line, the Tendring Hundred Railway which built from Colchester to Walton, completed in May 1867 which would effectively have taken away most of the traffic had the MTWR been completed. As it was, the independent Wivenhoe & Brightlingsea Railway was built as a branch of the THR from east of Wivenhoe, running along the Colne estuary just above the high tide mark into the ancient Cinque Port of Brightlingsea. There were no intermediate stations, few complications and the line opened to traffic on 18 April 1866.

Just before the opening of the railway to Brightlingsea,

Colchester acquired a new station much nearer the town centre at St Botolphs, a terminus used subsequently for Walton, Brightlingsea and later the local services to Clacton. Both on original plans and in actual construction the Eastern Counties Railway and the Eastern Union Railway had built stations well outside the towns they intended to serve, necessitating a long walk into the centre.

From Wivenhoe junction the route of the branch is along the shore of the estuary, one of the most important yachting centres in Essex. As the estuary widens before the line turns north-eastwards towards Brightlingsea town Mersea Island can be seen, on a bright summer's day a mixture of woods and arable fields across a stretch of blue water alive with sails. On a murky day at low tide a very different 'Whistleresque' view is seen. The land to the east of the line rises sharply to a rolling plateau now being rapidly built-up. The only engineering feature of note en route was the Alresford Swing Bridge across the Alresford Creek, necessary to give Thames barges passage to mills upstream. These barges remained strongly competitive with railways along the Essex and Suffolk coastal waterways until after World War II and can still be seen at Brightlingsea and Pin Mill on the Stour, where their present owners moor them between cruises. The swing bridge made a speed restriction of 10mph necessary and a pilotman was used to take trains over until LNER economies cut him out in 1925.

The original terminus had an overall roof in which the winds off the North Sea circulated mercilessly at most times of the year. It was burned down, not entirely to the sorrow of the inhabitants, on New Year's Eve 1901, being replaced with a simpler station which featured a run-round loop and abutted the fish loading dock at the buffer-stops. Only Hunstanton could rival Brightlingsea for immediacy to the seaside, but the former was not a fishing port while the latter had no beach, being mainly developed as a sailing centre when recreation became widespread in the late nineteenth century. Day trippers from Colchester and further afield also became an important traffic supplement. Amusements and walking along the wharves held their perennial fascination for townsfolk and with a boat trip thrown in, Brightlingsea was able to get a share of the seaside traffic, although never on the scale that Clacton achieved.

Mixed trains were common on the Brightlingsea branch and although in the early years of this century a wide variety of locomotives headed these trains, the whole range of 2–4–2 tanks have been seen at one time or another, together with E4s and the rebuilt D13s (T19s before rebuilding as 4–4–0s), but from the start of World War II the ubiquitous J15 took over until dieselisation. Two to three coaches plus any vans or trucks was the normal train, but the simple yet effective J15 was capable of taking anything from a single van to a long excursion train along the branch with equal aplomb.

It was with foreboding that railway enthusiasts heard the news of the East Coast floods in 1953. The great surge destroyed much of the waterside branch and closed the line for many months. Fears were expressed that the expected cost would be used as a reason for not reopening—many branches in East Anglia had recently closed and others were endangered —but on 7 December 1953, ten months and a week after the flood a four-coach train hauled by a J15 crept out of Brightlingsea at 6.40 am, whistle blasting and detonators exploding. The 'Crab & Winkle' was back in business again! With eleven trains a day and Sunday services the line did good business for a while. The station at Brightlingsea was convenient for the fish traffic and nearly every train at that time had a fish van attached. Class 2MT 2–6–0s appeared regularly together with new standard non-corridor stock, which was decidedly more comfortable than many of the decaying GER coaches then all too prevalent throughout East Anglia. Special cheap day and weekly tickets, excursions for local passengers to London and much local publicity helped greatly at this time. Brightlingsea was however growing outwards away from the railway station and for an increasing number of people the bus gave a shorter door-to-door timing on the short ride to Colchester which was the main destination. After three-and-a-half years of the new steam services, diesels took over in June 1957 with a further improved service, but traffic was tending to peak at rush hours and very few used the generous services at other times. The fish traffic was tending to go by road more and more frequently in the early 1960s, so that this line was an obvious candidate for closure in the massive abandonments of 1964.

Of all the longer east–west journeys across East Anglia that from Brightlingsea to Audley End would receive the highest commendation from my own point of view. The railway interest is outstanding, the scenery some of the best, many things for less enthusiastic members of the family to see and do on the way and visits for them to make while the railway enthusiast of the family potters around derelict stations or admires the brickwork on a redundant bridge. Station buildings provide a wide variety of interest. Attempts are being made to restore a section of the CVR and at the time of writing appear to be bearing fruit, with locomotives being regularly steamed by a friendly group at Chappel & Wakes Colne.

CHAPTER 9

Norfolk–Suffolk Borders

The border between Norfolk and Suffolk is marked by rivers which run along the route of a former glacial spillway, forming a wide marshy valley which beckoned invitingly to railway promoters as an easy routeway from west to east. The eastern sector of this valley contains the Waveney, and along this many projected railways were planned during the Railway Mania of the mid-1840s. The valley of the Little Ouse in the west was used by the Norfolk Railway for its main line from Norwich to Brandon and as such remains today as the first section of the route from East Anglia to the Midlands. Many people are surprised that in such a low-lying region as East Anglia easy routeways really matter, but a glance at the gradient profiles of the M&GN lines or the East Suffolk or even better a ride at the front of a diesel car on the East Norfolk line would soon convince them that earthworks can be substantially reduced and construction costs minimised when natural routeways are chosen.

Apart from the Waveney Valley Railway, three other short lines of great interest have now been abandoned. The Mellis to Eye branch was an attempt to bring the railway to a market town that the main line missed by a mere three miles, but even such a short distance was considered crucial to prosperity or lack of it in Victorian transport economics. The loop from Forncett to Wymondham avoided Norwich for traffic going through to North Norfolk and at one time boasted through carriages from express trains, but never really fulfilled its intended purpose. Finally there was the

Scole Railway near Diss, a private line whch served a market gardening estate in a manner well ahead of its time.

The penalties of being missed by the main line were exemplified at Eye more than in most East Anglian towns. The original Eastern Counties plan was to build the main Norwich to Ipswich line via Debenham and Eye, but when that curmugeon among early railways failed to build beyond Colchester, the Eastern Union Railway based on Ipswich

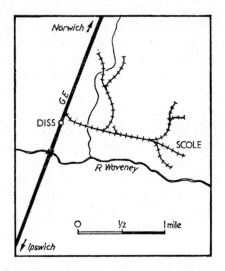

built a similar line but via Stowmarket and Diss. After nearly two decades the Mellis & Eye Railway was promoted by local interests and opened two years later in April 1867. It was a short, almost straight line curving away sharply from the main line and running directly to Eye with no intermediate station originally. The only feature of note was the crossing of the main road at the point where Yaxley Halt was opened a week before the Railway amalgamation. No engineering feats of note were needed. Eye station was a substantial set of buildings around the goods yard close to the town centre. The GER operated the line for fifty per cent of receipts, which do not seem to have been great. So obscure

Plates 25 and 26. Junctions and plain track. *Above:* Goods trains crossing at Bungay in 1950, hauled by Class J15 0–6–0 No 65433 and B12 4–6–0 No 61577. *Below:* Worlington Golf Links Halt, with Class E4 2–4–0 No 62781, in 1953. Today, the bridge remains above ploughed fields. *(Dr I. C. Allen)*

Plates 27 and 28. Small trains. *Above:* Class J15 0–6–0 No 65467 awaits a London connection at Haughley, junction for the Mid-Suffolk Light Railway. *Below:* On the Kelvedon & Tollesbury Light Railway Class J69 0–6–0T No 68616 is depicted near Tiptree in 1950, with two former Wisbech & Upwell bogie coaches in its train. *(Dr I. C. Allen)*

was the line that it was many years before the Board of
Trade noticed that no annual returns were being made, as
railways were bound to do in law. The company secretary
pleaded that the cost of printing this information was beyond
the meagre resources of the line and begged to be excused.
As returns were produced subsequently it seems that the
Board of Trade insisted. The population of Eye declined
almost continuously after the building of the railway and
finances were very weak. Eventually the GER took over the
line in its great tidying-up of 1898, continuing to run a
thin service, often of mixed trains, with few good express
connections. Conductor-guard trains, ancestors of the modern
Paytrain, failed to reduce costs sufficiently even with the
addition of traffic from the new halt at Yaxley, so that this
branch was one of the first victims of closure for passenger
services, on 2 February 1931. Bus services were direct to
larger centres; nevertheless the horse-and-cart mentality drew
farm traffic to railheads so that the goods services lasted until
13 July 1964. Diss, in contrast, has expanded; its station
and goods yards are still very busy and many London,
Ipswich and Norwich commuters now use that station daily.

Diss was itself once the junction for one of the very few
estate railways in East Anglia, the Scole Railway. The Frenze
Estate to the east of .Diss station was owned by a very
progressive landowner, William Betts, who saw the arrival
of the Eastern Union Railway at Diss in 1849 as a golden
opportunity to send his market gardening produce quickly
to the growing London markets. Never a man to do things by
halves he had seven miles of track of standard gauge built,
with a main line from a junction just north of the present
Diss station through to the village of Scole on the main road
with branches serving the Hall, brickfield and barn. One
might almost say he was a spiritual ancestor of Alan Bloom
who today farms and runs his railway system at Bressingham
a few miles west of Diss in the same Waveney valley. There
were two locomotives, a small 0–6–0 tank and an even

smaller 0–4–0 tank. They filled up with water at a tank which was supplied by pumps powered by a pair of traction engines. Operation was simply one engine in steam so there were no signalling or locking problems. Other rolling stock included fifteen wagons to Betts' own specification, which were loaded on the estate and then attached to London-bound trains at Diss. When the amount of produce for despatch exceeded their capacity, further wagons were hired from the ECR.

For thirty-five years the Scole Railway helped the Frenze Estate prosper. A pair of large brickfields opened and the variety of crops multiplied. Even passenger services for work-people and other locals started, using the trucks with planks instead of proper seats, this being permissible on a private estate line. Betts' death in 1885 led to the estate being divided and the integrity of the estate endangered. By that date expensive renewals were needed and the successors did not continue market gardening according to the Agricultural Returns, so there seems to have been a severe crisis which led to the dismantling of the line in 1886, only a year later. This was a lightly-laid line which for over three decades gave one of the most depressed areas in Norfolk a shining lead in what could be done to alleviate distress by capital investment in the farming business, using the latest methods of the time. Few others had the foresight of William Betts.

The railway which was planned in 1846 to start from Diss was the Waveney Valley Railway. From this junction it was proposed to build a line alongside the Waveney to serve Bungay, Beccles, Lowestoft and Yarmouth, giving these towns a more direct route to London than was available via Norwich and Cambridge. Nothing came of this and the inhabitants of Harleston, fearing that they might lack rail communication altogether, planned a line from Tivetshall Junction further north direct to their town. This was opened as the Waveney Valley Railway in 1855 and extended by stages slowly towards Bungay, five years after opening to

Harleston. Beccles was reached two-and-a-half years later, the line being opened on the very day that the WVR was formally merged with the GER. The two previous years were marked by a period of operation by the owning company, a fairly rare occurrence in East Anglia and usually unprofitable, as the local squires, merchants and bankers had little idea of detailed railway working, and even less of how to make a surplus on so rural a line which promised little as a through connection as rivals had already been built. They were in fact happy to be taken-over by the newly-reorganised monopoly company.

Except as a through route the Waveney Valley was poorly aligned for the main direction of local traffic, towards Norwich. Frequent level-crossings and only two small market towns en route proved inadequate passenger generators. Goods traffic was more substantial, especially in wartime, but the whole pace of the Waveney Valley was slow, with industries declining throughout most of the line's history. For the onlooker there was however one great compensation, the appearance of the stations was of the highest order. Flower beds, liberal use of whitewash and plenty of spit-and-polish explained the framed certificates in so many of the station booking halls, telling of station gardens competitions won on numerous occasions. The day when the inspection carriage was propelled along the line with the observation window to the fore was a key day in the railway year. Notes were taken, questions asked, pleasantries exchanged, then the party was off to the next station. Inspection on the Norwich Division was a very comfortable affair in the observation saloon with its grand view and deep cushioned chairs. In LNER days, William Whitelaw, father of the former Conservative Minister, regarded occasional visits like this as a good opportunity to get to know the staff, as well as being able to view the lines pleasantly. He would often combine such duties with attendance at a performance by a local railway drama group in the evening or a railway social. An alternative in some other divisions was a shielded bench bolted on to the front of an E4 which provided the inspecting team with a good if chilly view of rural stations.

The abandoned line which was once double and of main line status was the curve from Forncett to Wymondham. A combination of Charles Parkes' management and fear of M&GN encroachment and competition for traffic in North Norfolk led to the proposing of many curves, loops and more direct lines in the 1880s. East Dereham yards were extended at this time in expectation of traffic developing on the Western Extension of the East Norfolk Railway from Aylsham to County School. To avoid reversal at the busy Norwich junctions the Forncett to Wymondham line diverged from the Ipswich main line on the western side and ran in a broad curve via the only intermediate station, Ashwellthorpe, to approach Wymondham from the east, ready to continue directly on to the Wells and King's Lynn line. Had North Norfolk developed 'like a second Scarborough' in Charles Parkes' words there would have been much use made of this line, but in the event, only a single portion of a Liverpool Street–Norwich train was detached at Forncett for a few years around 1900 and continued slowly thence to East Dereham and Wells. Goods traffic was equally uninspiring in quantity so that although there was double track all the way on a direct line from London to East Dereham the traffic rarely justified it. The most important occasion when it did was in the aftermath of the great flood of 1912 when the line between Forncett and Norwich was out of action and even the 'Norfolk Coast Express' was diverted via Forncett and Wymondham without losing more than half an hour on its fast timing, despite reversal at Wymondham. Thus this relic of the great struggle for the North Norfolk seaside traffic which never quite lived up to the hopes of the promoters continued with local services until the start of World War II for passengers, closing on 10 September 1939, and with goods traffic until 4 August 1951. Since then the main view seen by passengers through Wymondham has been a curving line of carriages or locomotives destined for scrapping at King's of Norwich who use that end of the line for storage.

As Bressingham does not open until the afternoon, a profitable morning can be spent exploring the railway remains on the borders of Norfolk and Suffolk. Starting at Beccles, the Waveney Valley Railway is replete with station and crossing-keepers' houses, many in excellent condition. Only Bungay is being systematically erased. The buildings mostly date from the 1850s. Pulham Market and Harleston are the most rewarding to see, being both large and well-preserved. Ale enthusiasts will appreciate the proximity of maltings at Ditchingham and Tivetshall, both of which show clear signs of their former rail connections. Eye station buildings are still largely intact and the outlines of the former goods yard are clear, while the little town has enough sights and shops to keep other members of the family happy. Further north, Forncett offers one of the few visible turntable pits still to be seen, alongside the main line but intended to serve the branch. The bridge just north of the former station site spans the main line and the now empty curve of the line to Ashwellthorpe, a bridge typical of GER practice in the 1880s. Ashwellthorpe station is now a private house and well-preserved.

CHAPTER 10

Quayside Tramways and Other Minor Lines

East Anglia has a large number of small ports which receive coastal and continental traffic. In many cases small tramways from the railway down to the quayside were built from 1847 onwards so that transfer of goods was made easier and did not require the intermediate use of horse-and-cart. One of the King's Lynn lines and the GER quayside line at Ipswich remain as illustrations of past activity, but many such as those at Wells, Maldon, Lowestoft, Wisbech and Colchester have been swept away in the name of progress. While normal goods stock was used, the locomotives were usually special tramway types as used on the Wisbech & Upwell, the slightly more conventional 'Coffeepots', or yet the Sentinel geared locomotives of the inter-war period. Dock work was still important enough for specially designed diesel locomotives to be assigned to this work in the 1950s. Horses were commonly used where traffic was light and in the nineteenth century were mandatory where permission to operate steam locomotives was not granted.

The sight of a locomotive-hauled train proceeding along a public street or quay is unusual enough in this country to create a good deal of interest. Very stringent rules covered the use of such trains with a limitation of speed to walking pace, being preceded by a man with a red flag and the use of bell and other audible warnings.

One of the earliest of such lines ran from Yarmouth Vauxhall down to the Fish Quay. This was joined in 1882 by the Yarmouth Union Railway from the Beach station to a junction near Lacon's brewery stores, where the points can still be seen in the road surface. When the Great Yarmouth & Stalham (Light) Railway was built from Yarmouth in 1876 it was hoped to connect this line to the quayside and thereby to the GER at Vauxhall by means of a short tramway. The GER would have none of this and pointed to the gradient down to the proposed unsignalled junction which might have been a cause of accidents if any runaway trucks careered down the slope. The ulterior motive seems to have been to prevent the GYS(L)R achieving any through goods traffic of its own, and also to prevent it from abstracting any of the GER fish trade. These stalling tactics worked to the extent of delaying the development of goods traffic on the GYS(L)R by five years. Eventually arbitrators allowed the nominally-separate Yarmouth Union Railway to build a line from the GYS(L)R spur out of Yarmouth Beach station to link with the tramway after passing through the narrow defile between the 'White Swan' public house and neighbouring properties. Horses were to be used, but the Board of Trade had powers to sanction the use of steam locomotives later. Little interference was met from either pedestrians or wheeled traffic in the early days. A traffic census of 1880 shows only one hundred wheeled vehicles a day crossing the line. Nor need the GER have feared too much competition for its fish trade, as the YUR only carried 5,000 tons a year of it in the 1880s as against 55,000 tons by the GER.

In the twentieth century, the sight of a small tank engine puffing slowly across the road from behind a public house was always one to stop crowds of holidaymakers on their way to or from the other Yarmouth stations. The traffic was held at bay by the man with the red flag while the train was slowly eased across the points and along the quayside. There were more traffic delays at the busy Haven Bridge, and most people in a hurry reckoned the tramway a thorough nuisance. In later years, when car parking outgrew the capacity of the roadsides, especially in summer, motorists from outside Yarmouth often straddled the tracks unwittingly with their vehicles, others parked too near for safe clearance so that trains were slowed even more while owners were sought to move their offending possessions. One memorable trip of a mile-and-a-half took no less than seven hours one way!

The quayside line at Hythe, port of Colchester, was a stronghold of the tiny Neilson 'Coffeepot' locomotives adapted to tramway use by the provision of cowcatcher, skirting, dumb buffers and a spark-arresting chimney, while the tiny cab was crowned with a bell. So peculiar in appearance were these locomotives that the LNER used one of them to show alongside its latest products at exhibitions on a 'dignity and impudence' basis.

The tramway from Woodbridge to Sun Wharf near Melton was operated by a pair of magnificent shire horses until the late 1950s, a fine sight for passengers on the East Suffolk main line as the tramway ran alongside for some distance. Horse-shunting had been used on such lines in East Anglia for over a century and the last horse was only retired from shunting horse-boxes at Newmarket, very appropriately, as recently as 1967. After that the more aristocratic race horses travelled by road.

Lowestoft Fish Quay was reached by a short branch from the station which crossed the main A12 and generally the Sentinel- and later diesel-hauled trains caused traffic jams to develop, aided and abetted by the swing bridge a little further down the road, whose ability to jam was almost unrivalled in a region of swing bridges. Increasing road traffic has made such diversions economically harmful so their demise is not delayed or mourned in official circles.

Gazetteer

Detailed information on the lines noted in the text is given here, including opening and closing dates, dates of the relevant Acts of Parliament, changes in ownership, and the locations of the principal remains.

Some lines retain most of their stations and other lineside buildings, so I have picked only the best, or the most accessible. Elsewhere, almost all traces have been destroyed. In addition, there are constant demolitions, road schemes, and general decay, which will obliterate features noted during the survey. The details given here relate to the area as it was in 1975; I will be grateful to learn of changes as they occur.

During the preparation of this book the most dramatic post-war fuel crisis and inflation of transport costs has occurred, and although those holidaying by car may well wish to tour these sites by road, it is worth noting that the approach to many of them may be made more cheaply (especially for one or two people) by rail and bus. At the time of writing, the region was covered in summer by a weekly rail ticket costing £5.00, and a cycle could be taken for an extra £2.50. Delightful tours can be made, say, from March to Cambridge or Cromer to Yarmouth, going to or from base by train. The Eastern Counties bus company were offering daily tickets over all routes from Colchester northward and from Peterborough eastward for £1.05 per day, providing jumping-off points for exploration, or parallelling many routes. (The fares shown, are of course, liable to alteration.) A superficial tour by car can be made in each area in a day, but much longer is recommended; taking a day or so over a twenty-mile line would give the full flavour of line and district much better.

Essential equipment includes copies of the 1in or the new 1:50,000 Ordnance Survey sheets—both have their advantages. A 1950s edition will give the lines and all stations. The new 1:50,000 sheets are of variable accuracy: I have found items which had disappeared several years before the maps were printed clearly marked, while some very prominent items, like the bridge over the River Bure at Yarmouth do not appear. There is only one positive check, as I found out the hard way —go and see for yourself! You will also see much wonderful East Anglian countryside, traverse a natural historian's paradise in the many abandoned cuttings, and re-create the past as you journey.

The 1in O.S. sheets required are: 123, 124, 125, 126, 134, 135, 136, 137, 147, 148, 149, 150, 160, 161, and 162. For the 1:50,000 series, the numbers are: 131, 132, 133, 134, 142, 143, 144, 153, 154, 155, 156, 166, 167, 168, and 169.

The abbreviations in the side headings are:

ACT—date of Act of Parliament.
OPENED—opening dates of lines and types of services.
CLOSED—closing dates of lines and services affected.
REMAINS—remaining features of interest.
SETTING—type of landscape through which the line passes.
USES—present uses of buildings, trackbed, and other structures.

Other abbreviations are:

pass—passenger services.
gds—goods services.

CHAPTER 1: NORTH-EAST NORFOLK

NORTH WALSHAM–MUNDESLEY–CROMER BEACH   14½ miles
ACTS: Eastern & Midlands: North Walsham–Mundesley, 20 June 1888. Extended, transferred to M&GNR, Mundesley–Cromer: Norfolk & Suffolk Joint Committee, 5 July 1898.
OPENED: North Walsham–Mundesley: 20 June 1898 (*gds*); 1 July 1898 (*pass*). Mundesley–Cromer Beach: 3 August 1906 (*pass*); March 1907 (*gds*). Operated by M&GNJR with some GER trains, North Walsham Main–Mundesley. LNER operation after 1 October 1936. Incorporated into British Railways: 1 January 1948.
CLOSED: Cromer Beach–Mundesley: 17 April 1953 (*all*).
Newstead Lane–Runton West Jcn: 21 April 1963 (*all*).
North Walsham–Mundesley: 5 October 1964 (*pass*); 28 December 1964 (*gds*).

REMAINS: Earthworks and trackbed largely intact, also several bridges and abutments. Bridges at 285315 and 278383 worth seeing as typical of the two construction phases. Paston & Knapton (312342) and Overstrand stations still intact. Platelayers' hut (292324). Ballast of Kelling Heath gravels and slag mixture can be seen near all above points.

USES: Pipeline buried under trackbed from North Walsham to near Mundesley for Bacton Gas Terminal. Mundesley and Trimingham station sites now housing estates. Paston & Knapton and Overstrand stations now private dwellings. Piggery on trackbed at 312358. By-pass at North Walsham (282301).

MELTON CONSTABLE–NORTH WALSHAM–YARMOUTH BEACH   41½ miles

ACTS: Yarmouth & Stalham (Light) Railway: Yarmouth–Stalham, 26 July 1876; Stalham–North Walsham, 27 May 1878. Lynn & Fakenham Act, 11 August 1881: Melton Constable–North Walsham.

OPENED: Yarmouth Beach–Ormesby, 7 August 1877; Ormesby–Hemsby, 16 May 1878; Hemsby–Martham: 15 July 1878; Martham–Catfield: 17 January 1880; Catfield–Stalham: 3 July 1880; Stalham–North Walsham: 13 June 1881; North Walsham–Melton Constable: 5 April 1883.

Incorporated in Yarmouth & North Norfolk (Light) Railway: 27 May 1878; Eastern & Midlands Railway: 1 January 1883; M&GNR: 1 July 1893.

CLOSED: 2 March 1959 (*all*) except North Walsham Town goods yard and newly-built junction with GER line. Track lifted 1967.

REMAINS: Numerous stations, bridges and abutments as well as earthworks between Melton Constable and Stalham. Yarmouth Beach, Ormesby, Martham, Stalham, Bluestone, Felmingham and Corpusty stations partly or wholly intact. Trackbed is easily followed from Melton Constable to Stalham, most bridges intact and Kelling Heath ballast prevents undergrowth. Several concrete overbridges between Yarmouth and Caister. Double-track bridge at Briston (059322) worth seeing for E&M and M&GNJR structures alongside each other. Single-line bridges at 251286 and 306275 are more typical. Crossing keeper's cottage, of standard type, at Tungate (269295) is well preserved. Melton Constable station has been demolished but platforms remain.

USES: Stalham to Potter Heigham Bridge used as a by-pass, concrete bridge on site of old swing bridge. Yarmouth Beach is a coach station and car park. Stalham and Martham stations and yards are road depots. Ormesby station is a private house (499149). North Walsham Town station site is now used as a new sewage unit while Corpusty station buildings form an amenity block for a summer camp. Some house building over the track between Yarmouth and Hemsby and demolition of stations and structures. Section from Oulton airfield (139266) and Abel Heath (172269) completely reclaimed for farming. Cutting east of Abel Heath being infilled with rubbish and soil.

MELTON CONSTABLE–NORWICH   21½ miles
Lynn & Fakenham Railway
ACT: 12 August 1880.
OPENED: Melton Constable–Guestwick: 19 January 1882; Guestwick–Lenwade: 1 July 1882; Lenwade–Norwich City: 2 December 1882.
Incorporated in E&MR: 1 January 1883; M&GNR: 1 July 1893.
CLOSED: Melton Constable–Norwich City: 2 March 1959 (*pass*). Melton Constable–Themelthorpe: 2 March 1959 (*gds*); Lenwade–Norwich City: 12 September 1960 (*gds*). Line between Themelthorpe and Lenwade still used for Anglian Concrete Products.
REMAINS: Most stations and crossing keepers' cottages intact—several of the latter made of concrete blocks. Fencing in typical M&GNJR style. Overbridge at Themelthorpe across GER (058202). Walls of City goods yard and stub of platform (225093). Unique 'A'-frame bridges at Mile Cross (221099), Hellesdon (198099) and Drayton (179132) over the Wensum. Pre-stressed concrete footbridge (220099) shows versatility of the medium.
USES: Norwich City now the City Industrial Estate, also possible route of new road. A furniture hypermarket has been built on the City station site. Walk planned alongside the river to Drayton. Guestwick station now a fine private house retaining many original architectural features. Attlebridge is a factory, as was Hellesdon until mid-1974. Crossing keepers' cottages occupied as private dwellings.
SETTING: Mid-Norfolk arable country from Melton Constable

to Whitwell & Reepham then Wensum valley and wooded heathland alternating to the approaches to City station. Particularly picturesque between Drayton and Hellesdon.

MELTON CONSTABLE–SHERINGHAM   11½ miles
ACTS: Melton Constable–Kelling: 12 August 1880; Kelling–Sheringham: 1884, Cromer Undertaking.
OPENED: Melton Constable–Holt: 1 October 1884; Holt–Cromer: 16 June 1887. Incorporated in E&MR: 1 January 1883; whole line absorbed into M&GNR: 1 July 1893.
CLOSED: Melton Constable–Sheringham: 6 April 1964 (*pass*); 28 December 1964 (*gds*).
Line between Sheringham Halt (other side of road from original Sheringham station) and Cromer open for Paytrains. Line between Sheringham station and Weybourne open on summer weekends for North Norfolk Railway steam trains, operated by and for members—instant membership available.
REMAINS: Heavy earthworks and bridges largely intact between Melton Constable and Weybourne; rest of the line in operating order. Good overbridge at 077384. Parts of platform only at Holt (082385). Weybourne and Sheringham stations well worth visiting, woodwork of the former particularly good, many relics in the exhibition at Sheringham besides mobile exhibits, signalling equipment and photographs.
USES: Holt station site in course of redevelopment. New alignment of main road at 095395.
SETTING: Steep descent and climb with 1 in 80 gradients from Melton Constable to Holt across the very picturesque hilly countryside. Curves sinuously across the open heathland of Kelling (look out for old railway quarries which supplied ballast for track and for concrete structures). At 106418 the line emerges from a cutting giving a breathtaking view of Weybourne mill set on the edge of the North Norfolk coast.

WESTERN EXTENSION–EAST NORFOLK RAILWAY
East Norfolk Railway   9 miles. Reepham to County School
ACT: July 1879. 43–4 Vic. Ch cxxxvi.
OPENED: Final section: 1 May 1882.
Incorporated into GER: 1882. Worked from outset by GER, and largely financed by GER.
CLOSED: Reepham–County School: 15 September 1952 (*pass*). Reepham–Foulsham: 15 September 1952 (*gds*). Reinstated as

light railway, Reepham–Themelthorpe Curve (063242): 12 September 1960 (*gds*). County School–Foulsham: 31 October 1964 (*gds*).

REMAINS: Earthworks at Broom Green (north of County School) and Themelthorpe. Foulsham station buildings and platform (027243).

USES: Foulsham now a private house and coalyard, trackbed is a garden.

SETTING: Meander of the Wensum at junction, then arable mid-Norfolk plateau to Aylsham. Bure valley from Aylsham to Wroxham is the most picturesque part of the original through line.

CROMER JUNCTION–CROMER HIGH   1 mile
East Norfolk Railway
ACT: 1872, 38–9 Vic. Ch xvii.
OPENED: 26 March 1877.
Incorporated into GER 1882. Operated by GER from outset.
CLOSED: 20 September 1954 (*pass*); 7 March 1960 (*gds*).
REMAINS: Cutting from the former junction. N&SJRC tunnel under trackbed. Cromer High station demolished.
SETTING: Perched on the lip of the escarpment at the edge of the Cromer–Holt Moraine. A monument to the inability of the ENR to engineer a station nearer the town.

CHAPTER 2: MID-ESSEX AND NORTH-EAST HERTFORDSHIRE

WITHAM–MALDON   5¾ miles
Maldon, Witham & Braintree Railway
ACT: 1846, 9–10 Vic. Ch lii.
OPENED: 15 August 1848 (*gds*); 2 October 1848 (*pass*).
Incorporated into Eastern Counties Railway 1846.
CLOSED: 7 September 1964 (*pass*); 18 April 1966 (*gds*).
REMAINS: Earthworks and several bridges including A12 Witham by-pass. Maldon station (852077) is architecturally interesting example of 1840s station. Branch platform at Witham.
USES: Sidings at Witham on original branch.
SETTING: Lower valley of River Blackwater leading to ancient seaport through orchard country.

WOODHAM FERRERS–MALDON   8¾ .miles
Great Eastern Railway, New Essex line
ACT: 1883.
OPENED: 1 October 1889.
Incorporated into LNER: 1 January 1923.
CLOSED: Triangular junctions at Witham and Maldon: end summer season 1895 (*pass*). 10 September 1939 (remaining *pass*). Woodham Ferrers–Maldon West: 1 April 1953 (*gds*); Maldon East–Maldon West: 31 January 1959 (*gds*).
REMAINS: Earthworks largely intact including triangular junction at Maldon. Cuttings filled with woodland and bridges mostly gone except at 846025.
USES: Linear housing estate at Cold Norton (850005). Linear woodland from Cold Norton to Woodland Ferrers and from Maldon West to Purleigh in the cuttings. Farm track uses trackbed at 845025.

KELVEDON–TOLLESBURY PIER   10¼ miles
Kelvedon, Tiptree & Tollesbury Pier Light Railway
ACT: Light Railway Order, 1901.
OPENED: Kelvedon–Tollesbury: 1 October 1904; Tollesbury–Tollesbury Pier: 15 May 1907.
Incorporated into LNER: 1 January 1923.
CLOSED: Tollesbury–Tollesbury Pier: 17 July 1921 (*all*). Used again for mobile guns 1939–40. Kelvedon–Tollesbury: 7 May 1951 (*pass*); Tollesbury–Tudwick Road: 29 October 1951 (*gds*); Kelvedon–Tudwick Road: 10 October 1962 (*gds*).
REMAINS: Part of earthworks from Kelvedon station, for 200 metres. Embankment and conduit at Domsey Brook (873189). Earthworks south of Tiptree. Traces of pier extension on Tollesbury Wick Marshes (9709XX).
USES: Housing estate at Kelvedon. Farm track from Tolleshunt Knights (926139) to Bourchier's Hall (951119).

ELSENHAM–THAXTED   5½ miles
Elsenham & Thaxted Light Railway
ACT: Light Railway Order: 1906.
OPENED: 1 April 1913.
Incorporated in LNER: 1 January 1923.
CLOSED: 15 September 1952 (*pass*); 1 June 1953 (*gds*).
REMAINS: Branch platform can be distinguished at Elsenham.

Minor cutting just discernible at 588301, where it is marked by a track.

USES: Largely returned to arable farming.

SETTING: Runs along the interfluve between Thames and Ouse basins, over 100 metres above sea level (330ft) most of the way.

BISHOP'S STORTFORD–DUNMOW–BRAINTREE 18 miles
Bishop's Stortford, Dunmow & Braintree Railway
ACT: 22 July 1861.
OPENED: 22 February 1869.
Vested in GER: 22 February 1869.
CLOSED: 3 March 1952 (*pass*, except occasional excursions).
Felstead–Dunmow: 18 April 1966 (*gds*); Braintree–Felstead, regular services Bishop's Stortford–Dunmow: 1 April 1969 (*gds*).
REMAINS: Road and river bridges at Great Dunmow. Numerous light earthworks throughout. Station at Takely.
SETTING: Crosses mid-Essex plateau at right-angles to drainage. Boulder clay farmland.

ST MARGARET'S–BUNTINGFORD 13¾ miles
Ware, Hadham & Buntingford Railway
ACT: 12 July 1858.
OPENED: 3 July 1863.
Purchased by GER: 1 September 1868.
CLOSED: 16 November 1964 (*pass*). 20 September 1965 (*gds*).
REMAINS: Earthworks and many bridges throughout. Widford (407158) retains platform and signalbox. Standon (395225) is a good example of a weatherboard station; also the branch terminal at Buntingford (365288).
USES: Road widening of A10 at Westmill has removed some earthworks. Buntingford is now an office. Much of the trackbed ploughed-over around Hadham.
SETTING: Hertfordshire outer commuter belt. Sylvan valley in the chalklands.

HATFIELD–HERTFORD 9 miles
Hertford & Welwyn Junction Railway
ACT: 1854, 21–2 Vic. Ch xxiv.
OPENED: 1 March 1858.

Plates 29 and 30. Two views on the Kelvedon & Tollesbury Railway. *Above:* Tollesbury station looking towards the pier, photographed in May 1935. *Below:* Kelvedon low level station in August 1950. *(L&GRP)*

Plates 31 and 32.
Right: Typical station oil lamp, at one time found all over East Anglia. *Below:* Haughley Junction with a train departing for Norwich; the Bury line is on the left and the Mid-Suffolk Light curving away to the right. (*J. Watling, Dr I. C. Allen*)

Amalgamated with Luton, Dunstable & Welwyn Junction to form Hertford, Luton & Dunstable Railway on 28 June 1858. Absorbed by GNR on 12 June 1861.

CLOSED: 18 June 1951 (*pass*). Hertingfordbury–Hertford: 18 June 1951 (*gds*); Cole Green–Hertingfordbury: 5 March 1962 (*gds*). Remainder of line: 23 May 1966 (*gds*).

REMAINS: Earthworks visible throughout, several bridges beyond Cole Green. Hatfield to Welwyn section is now part of the main line. Cole Green station (283112).

USES: Housing covers former trackbed in Hertford.

SETTING: Welwyn Garden City, an inter-war new town, then heavily-wooded country above Mimram valley to old market town of Hertford.

CHAPTER 3: NORTH-WEST NORFOLK

KING'S LYNN–HUNSTANTON   15 miles
Lynn & Hunstanton Railway
ACT: 1 August 1861.
OPENED: 3 October 1862.

Merged with West Norfolk Junction Railway, 1874, forming Hunstanton & West Norfolk Railway. Absorbed by GER: 1 July 1890.

CLOSED: 28 December 1964 (*gds*); 5 May 1969 (*pass*).

REMAINS: Earthworks at Sandringham and west of Snettisham. Heacham Junction (668375), carstone (local ginger-coloured sandstone) station house with verandah intact as well as west platform and signalbox. Snettisham station buildings and goods shed (677335) and Dersingham station (681308). North Wootton (637244) intact but derelict. Wolferton (657282) is the best preserved with platforms, royal waiting rooms, signal-box and gates all intact and in good condition.

USES: Hunstanton station site redeveloped as resort extension (fun fair) and car park (672407). Caravan park along trackbed south of Heacham. Snettisham, Dersingham and Wolferton are private houses.

SETTING: Runs mostly between Wash shoreline and heath-lands of the Norfolk greensand around Sandringham. Often reclaimed marsh to seaward.

WELLS–BURNHAM MARKET–HEACHAM JUNCTION   18¾ miles
West Norfolk Junction Railway

ACT: 23 June 1864.
OPENED: 17 August 1866.
Merged with Lynn & Hunstanton Railway, 1874, forming Hunstanton & West Norfolk Railway. Absorbed by GER: 1 July 1890.
CLOSED: 12 June 1952 (*pass*). Burnham Market–Wells: 30 January 1953 (*gds*—not re-opened after flood damage, except for drainage trains); Heacham–Burnham Market: 28 December 1964 (*gds*).
REMAINS: Earthworks largely intact, but bridges usually down except for overbridge at Wells (922431). Burnham Market station intact with 0–6–0T *Rhos* (Hudswell Clarke 1918) at platform. Goods shed and LNER-style strip lights used. Stanhoe (798386), Docking (767378) and Sedgeford (712375) are all intact. Wooden signal frame, waiting room and goods shed also at Docking. Stanhoe still has its station signs and lamps. Sedgeford still has its level-crossing gates, nameboard and awning. All are in a very good state and are the best preserved set of branch-line stations in Norfolk, retaining the rural atmosphere. Well worth a visit.
USES: Stations are dwelling houses except for Burnham Market which is a garage with goods-shed as workshop. Holkham to Dale Hole (873442) section used as farm road. Wells has been developed as a small industrial estate and bus station.
SETTING: An unspoilt downland from Heacham to Burnham Market, then marshes with dunes to north and low degraded cliffs to the south, skirting the edge of Holkham beach.

WELLS–FAKENHAM   9½ miles
Wells & Fakenham Railway
ACT: 24 July 1854.
OPENED: 1 December 1857.
Incorporated in GER: 7 August 1862.
CLOSED: 5 October 1964 (*pass*); 31 October 1964 (*gds*).
REMAINS: Earthworks, bridges and trackbed largely intact. Walsingham (932367) and Wighton Halt (936395) are intact. Wighton one of very few abandoned halts still to be seen. Wells station house intact, but rest largely gone.
USES: Walsingham is a Russian Orthodox monastery, with a golden cupola. Wells Junction is a playing field. Wighton station house now private.
SETTING: Stiffkey valley is pleasantly hilly with picturesque

villages and outstanding churches; the trip can be combined with visits to the Walsingham shrines.

THETFORD–WATTON–SWAFFHAM   22¾ miles
Thetford & Watton Railway
Watton & Swaffham Railway
ACTS: Thetford & Watton: 16 July 1866.
Watton & Swaffham: 20 July 1869.
OPENED: Roudham–Watton: 28 January 1869 (*gds*), 18 October 1969 (*pass*).
Swaffham–Watton: 20 September 1875 (*gds*), 15 November 1875 (*pass*).
Incorporated in GER: 1898.
CLOSED: 15 June 1964 (*pass*). Thetford–Watton: 15 June 1964 (*gds*); Swaffham–Watton: 19 April 1965 (*gds*).
REMAINS: Earthworks abundant north of Watton. Stow Bedon (942965) intact but soon to be demolished. Wretham & Hockham station intact (917912). Good example of crossing keeper's cottage at Hipkin's Farm (937985).
USES: Industrial estate in Watton station yard (923006). New by-pass being built from Stow Bedon station to Wretham & Hockham. Latter station has a fine black flint house with garden beyond lip of platform.
SETTING: Watton to Thetford is across a sandy heath dotted with Scots pines, typical of the Brecklands. This is plateau country with sheep grazing (unusual in Norfolk) and the army battlegrounds. Forestry Commission plantations provide a further sombre backcloth.

MELTON CONSTABLE–FAKENHAM–KING'S LYNN   33¾ miles
Lynn & Fakenham Railway
ACTS: King's Lynn–Fakenham: 13 July 1876.
Fakenham–Melton Constable: 12 August 1880.
OPENED: King's Lynn–Massingham: 16 August 1879. Massingham–Fakenham: 6 August 1880. Fakenham–Melton Constable: 19 January 1882.
Incorporated into Eastern & Midlands Railway: 1 January 1883.
M&GNR from 1 July 1893.
CLOSED: 2 March 1959 (*pass*). East Rudham–Melton Constable: 2 March 1959 (*gds*); South Lynn–East Rudham: 1 May 1969 (*gds*).

REMAINS: Melton Constable works, the main erecting shops, offices, water tower and part of the tramway (narrow-gauge) around the works. All the main features of the original railway town housing are intact and the original 'Hastings Arms', schools and Railway Mission. This must be seen; there is nothing else like it in East Anglia. Thursford (867275) has goods shed and yard; Raynham Park (838263) intact including signalbox; East Rudham (995335), station and Melton Constable, cast concrete goods shed with cast-iron crane and height gauge, unusually complete. Massingham (793249) and Hillington (722252) are largely complete, latter with awning. Langor Bridge signalbox (96129).

USES: Melton Constable now an industrial estate; Thursford is a concrete products store; Raynham Park is a farm merchants' store; Massingham and Hillington are private houses, the latter being the Royal station for Sandringham of the M&GNJR. Langor Bridge to Manor cottages is a road and also part of the trackbed at Thursford.

SETTING: The line descends from the highest part of Norfolk down the western spur of the Cromer–Holt ridge and then along the Wensum valley from Langor Bridge to Raynham Park via Fakenham; this is particularly picturesque. Open chalkland is then crossed to Hillington where the heathland of plantations, gorse and rhododendrons is interspersed with farmland.

GAYWOOD JUNCTION–BAWSEY 3¼ miles
Lynn & Fakenham Railway
ACT: 13 July 1876.
OPENED: 16 August 1879.
Incorporated into Eastern & Midlands Railway: 1 January 1883.
CLOSED: 1 January 1886.
USES: Farm track from Waveland Farm to 665210. Pylons follow the last mile to Gaywood Junction (632211).
SETTING: Greensand heaths and woods descending to broad flat valley of Gaywood River.

LYNN LOOP LINE 4¾ miles
Eastern & Midlands Railway
ACT: 10 August 1882.
OPENED: 1 November 1885 (*gds*); 1 January 1886 (*pass*).

CLOSED: 2 March 1959 (*pass*); 1 May 1968 (*gds*).
REMAINS: Western end of line used for sugar-beet trains to Saddlebow factory. Earthworks still easily visible at eastern end.
USES: Lynn southern by-pass.
SETTING: As for Bawsey line.

KING'S LYNN–SWAFFHAM–DEREHAM   26½ miles
Lynn & Dereham Railway
ACT: 21 July 1845.
OPENED: Lynn to Narborough: 27 October 1846.
Narborough to Swaffham: 10 August 1847.
Swaffham to Sporle: 26 October 1847.
Sporle to Dereham: 11 September 1848.
Incorporated in East Anglian Railway: 1847; in GER: 1862.
CLOSED: 30 June 1966 (*gds*—except King's Lynn–Middleton).
9 September 1968 (*pass*).
REMAINS: Lynn to Middleton open for sand trains. Heavy cuttings through the chalk east of Narborough (744130). Level-crossing cottage in local carstone and platelayers' hut at West Bilney (725152). Narborough and East Winch (700169) worth seeing for local architecture. To be demolished if by-pass scheme goes through.
USES: Middleton to Swaffham to be used as new A47 road. Rubbish tip in deep cutting (804095).
SETTING: Low drained land below higher land from King's Lynn to Narborough then chalk escarpment of the East Anglian Heights to attain the boulder clay plateau beyond Swaffham.

CHAPTER 4: THE FENS
HOLME–RAMSEY   5¾ miles
Ramsey Railway
ACT: 1861. 24–5 Vic. Ch cxciv.
OPENED: 22 July 1863.
Transferred to GER: 1867. Incorporated in GER: 1875, Leased to and operated by GNR.
CLOSED: 6 October 1947 (*pass*); December 1973 (*gds*).
REMAINS: Station and track still intact late 1974.
SETTING: Crosses open fenland throughout.

SOMERSHAM–RAMSEY   7 miles
Ramsey & Somersham Railway

ACT: 2 June 1865.
OPENED: 16 September 1889.
Incorporated in GN&GE Joint Committee: 1 January 1897.
CLOSED: 22 September 1930. (*pass*—apart from occasional
excursions); Warboys–Ramsey: September 1956 (*gds*); Somersham–Warboys: 13 July 1964 (*gds*).
REMAINS: Ramsey (East) station (285848) weighbridge and
shed and also goods shed. Level-crossing keeper's cottage, gate-
posts and rails across Warboys–Chatteris road at 323807.
USES: Ramsey (East) site is now a concrete products factory
and small industrial estate. Bridge at 286845 used to connect
two parts of Ramsey golf course.
SETTING: Rolling countryside of a fen island; complete
contrast to Holme–Ramsey branch. The town of Ramsey is
very pleasant, ancient church and tree-lined greens.

ST IVES–ELY   17¾ miles
Ely, Haddenham & Sutton Railway
ACTS: 23 June 1864.
St Ives to Sutton: 1876.
OPENED: Ely–Sutton: 16 April 1866; St Ives–Sutton: 10 May
1878.
Incorporated into GER in 1898.
CLOSED: 2 February 1931 (*pass*—except excursions); 1957
(excursions).
Bluntisham Sutton: 6 October 1958 (*gds*); Ely–Sutton: 13
July 1964 (*gds*); St Ives–Bluntisham: 5 October 1964 (*gds*).
REMAINS: Trackbed is easiest to follow from Wilburton
(484764) to St Ives where by-roads and west of Earith light
earthworks mark the course. Stations at Stretham (515764),
Wilburton (484764) and Sutton (453785) give a good idea of
the architecture.
USES: Orchard at Bluntisham (355750). Roads on former trackbed from Sutton and Wilburton.
SETTING: The line follows a sinuous course between Fen
islands, largely avoiding earthworks and serving the largest
number of communities, but often at a distance from towns
and villages.

WISBECH–UPWELL   7¾ miles
Wisbech & Upwell Tramway, Great Eastern Railway
ACT: 1882.

OPENED: Wisbech–Outwell: 20 August 1883; to Upwell: 8 September 1884.
CLOSED: 2 January 1928 (*pass*); 23 May 1966 (*gds*).
REMAINS: Small brick depot buildings at Boyce's Bridge and Elm Bridge (473075).
USES: Road-widening at points throughout. Wisbech station demolished and redeveloped partly as an old folks' home.
SETTING: Winding road alongside largely infilled canal through rich orchards and market gardens.

THREE HORSESHOE JUNCTION–BENWICK GOODS   5 miles
Great Eastern Railway
ACT: Light Railway Order 1896.
OPENED: 2 August 1898.
CLOSED: 13 July 1964.
REMAINS: small sheds at Benwick (342907), White Fen (337923), Jones' Drove (338931), Burnt House (342937) and Quaker's Drove (344960). Trackbed mostly reclaimed. Bridge across Whittlesey Dike (343938).
USES: Store sheds built in Benwick station yard.
SETTING: Open fenland with only one hamlet, Benwick.

WISBECH–MAGDALEN ROAD   11¾ miles
East Anglian Railway
ACT: 30 June 1845.
OPENED: 1 February 1848.
Incorporated into GER 7 August 1862.
CLOSED: 5 October 1964 (*gds*); 9 September 1968 (*pass*).
REMAINS: Light earthworks at bridge approaches between Middle Drove and Magdalen Road. Bridges at 567101 and across Ouse at Magdalen Road. Most cottages and stations still intact.
USES: Cottages and station houses as private dwellings, bridges used by farm vehicles.
SETTING: Open fenland crossed by embanked rivers and straight roads. Orchard country approaching Wisbech.

ST IVES–CHATTERIS–MARCH   15½ miles
Wisbech, St Ives and Cambridge Junction Railway
ACT: 1846, 9–10 Vic. Ch ccclvi.
OPENED: 1 February 1848.

Incorporated in Eastern Counties Railway: 1847. GER from 7 August 1862.

GN&GER Joint Railway from 1882.

CLOSED: Spur to Chatteris Dock: 16 December 1955 (gds); 18 April 1966 (gds); 6 March 1967 (pass).

REMAINS: Wimblington (417925) has 1½ platforms and a crossing keeper's cottage. At Chatteris (387861) station platform and parts of the yard. Somersham (366777) is the most complete with old station lamps and station buildings with awnings. Trackbed can usually be followed. Earthworks south of Somersham intact and bridge over 40ft drain (385882).

USES: Paved road at Wimblington; road maintenance depot at Chatteris station.

SETTING: Fen island from St Ives to Somersham, many orchards alongside then open arable fenland to March.

DENVER–ABBEY–STOKE FERRY   7¾ miles
Downham & Stoke Ferry Railway
ACT: 21 July 1879.
OPENED: 1 August 1882.
Absorbed by GER: 1 January 1898.
CLOSED: 22 September 1930 (pass); Abbey–Stoke Ferry: 19 April 1965 (gds).
REMAINS: Stoke Ferry station (707907), crossing keeper's cottage at Wretton (686995).
USES: Cottage is a private residence. Denver to Abbey is used for trains serving Wissington.
SETTING: Skirts the edge of the black peat fens and the greensand alongside the new cut-off channel to Denver Sluice.

WISSINGTON RAILWAY   18 miles
ACT: (Private land.)
OPENED: 1906.
Taken over by British Sugar Corporation after 1925; Ministry of Agriculture from March 1941, who purchased it in 1947.
CLOSED: Lines beyond sugar beet factory: 30 June 1957.
REMAINS: Lines around sugar beet factory still in use.
USES: Reverted to farmland.
SETTING: Level peat fen.

SUTTON BRIDGE–WISBECH–PETERBOROUGH   28½ miles
Peterborough, Wisbeach (sic) & Sutton Railway

ACT: 28 July 1863.

OPENED: 1 June 1866 (*gds*); 1 August 1866 (*pass*).

Incorporated in E&MR: 1 July 1883; in M&GNJR: 1 July 1893.

CLOSED: 2 March 1959 (*pass*); Sutton Bridge–Wisbech: 2 March 1959 (*gds*); Eye Green–Peterborough: 2 March 1959 (*gds*); Murrow–Wisbech: 28 December 1964 (*gds*); Eye Green–Murrow: 20 July 1966 (*gds*).

REMAINS: Most stations intact and Murrow signalbox at former level crossing of GN&GEJR line (367065). Station house and goods shed only at Sutton Bridge (479210). Earthworks at approach to Peterborough New England (182015) Traces of extensive sidings at Eye brickworks (225028).

USES: Wisbech station is now a garage. Sutton Bridge goods shed is a Michelin tyre depot. Much of the line under the plough.

SETTING: Alongside the Nene dikes Sutton Bridge to Wisbech, orchard land to St Mary's arable fen to Eye then brickfields to Peterborough.

SOUTH LYNN–SUTTON BRIDGE–SPALDING   27¼ miles

Norwich & Spalding Railway

Lynn & Sutton Bridge Railway

ACTS: Spalding–Holbeach: 4 August 1853; Holbeach–Sutton Bridge: 13 August 1859; Lynn–Sutton Bridge: 6 August 1861.

OPENED: Spalding to Sutton Bridge: 3 July 1862; Lynn to Sutton Bridge: 1 March 1865.

Incorporated into Midland & Eastern Railway: 23 July 1866; amalgamated with lines east of Lynn to form Eastern & Midlands Railway: 1 July 1883; M&GNJR from 1 July 1893.

CLOSED: 2 March 1959 (*pass*). Spalding–Sutton Bridge: 1 May 1965 (*gds*); South Lynn–Sutton Bridge: 2 March 1961 (*gds*).

REMAINS: Most station buildings and crossing keepers' cottages still remain. Terrington (552191) is in particularly good order and representative of many. Rail/road swing bridge at Cross Keys (482210) is worth detailed examination.

USES: Station houses and crossing keepers' cottages in use as private residences. Goods sheds as stores. A few hundred yards of rail track at South Lynn connect the sugar factory with GER line. Parallel with this part of trackbed and Ouse bridge site are used for new southern by-pass with extension along track towards Sutton Bridge under consideration.

SETTING: Silt fen with intensive vegetable, flower and fruit growing. Towns and long villages along track almost throughout.

CUCKOO JUNCTION–WELLAND BANK (SPALDING AVOIDING LINE)   ¾ mile
Eastern & Midlands Railway
(Completed by M&GNJR.)
ACT: Midland Railway, 25 July 1890.
OPENED: 5 June 1893 (*gds*); 1 May 1894 (*pass*).
CLOSED: 2 March 1959 (*all*). Little used in previous three years.
REMAINS: Embankments.

LITTLE BYTHAM JUNCTION–BOURNE–SPALDING   14½ miles
Spalding & Bourne Railway
Eastern & Midlands Railway
ACTS: Spalding–Bourne: 29 July 1862.
Bourne–Little Bytham: 28 June 1888.
OPENED: Spalding–Bourne: 1 August 1866. Bourne–Little Bytham: 1 May 1893 (*gds*); 1 May 1894 (*pass*).
Incorporated in M&GNJR: 1 July 1893.
CLOSED: 2 March 1959. Bourne–Little Bytham: 2 March 1959 (*gds*); Spalding–Bourne: 5 April 1965 (*gds*).
REMAINS: Crossing keeper's cottage south of Moulton (305234) and Whaplode station house (325420) are typical of this section. Heavy earthworks west of Bourne where the line rises on to the Jurassic rocks after leaving the Fens. Spalding station still used for Ely–Doncaster and Spalding–Peterborough trains.
SETTING: Western Fens and a limestone ridge. Trip can be combined with Spalding Flower Festival to see countryside at its best.

EDENHAM & LITTLE BYTHAM RAILWAY   4 miles
Edenham & Little Bytham Railway
ACT: Private railway of Lord Willoughby de Eresby, 1856.
OPENED: 1856.
CLOSED: 17 October 1871 (*pass*—locomotive beyond repair).
1885 (*gds*—horses used until closure).
REMAINS: Bridge over stream at 022173.
USE: Unmetalled road (037189).

CHAPTER 5: EAST SUFFOLK

SOUTHWOLD–HALESWORTH   9 miles
Southwold Railway
ACT: 24 July 1876.
OPENED: 24 September 1879.
CLOSED: 12 April 1929.
REMAINS: Site of station yard at Halesworth alongside GER
station. Bridge abutments across main road (392776). Over-
bridge at Holton (405771). Approaches to Blyth swing bridge
(494757). Trackbed can be followed near Holton and most
of the way from Blower's Common to Southwold (535753 to
505765).
USES: Trackbed used as a farm track around Blythburgh church.
Bridleway from east of Blythburgh to Walberswick Common.
Bailey bridge across Blyth on the site of the former swing
bridge (494757). Fire station on site of Southwold station
(505765). Roadway along most of the harbour branch trackway
at Southwold.
SETTING: Valley of the Blyth from head of navigation at
Halesworth to the sea. The valley is typically broad and
marshy with a narrow river from Halesworth to Blythburgh,
then there is a broad estuary with heronry. The railway largely
followed the south bank travelling through heathland from
Blythburgh to the former Blyth swing bridge.

BENTLEY–CAPEL–HADLEIGH   7¼ miles
Eastern Union & Hadleigh Junction Railway
ACT: 1846, 9–10 Vic. Ch liii.
OPENED: 21 August 1847 (*gds*); 2 September 1847 (*pass*).
Incorporated into the Eastern Union Railway: 1848; GER
from 7 August 1862.
CLOSED: 29 February 1932 (*pass*—except for occasional excursions). 19 September 1965 (*gds*).
REMAINS: Platform and base of the station house at Capel
(103388) alongside the A12. Raydonwood station (059405)
with platform intact. Bridge at Wenham over a small stream
(075398) is typical of the lightly-built line and can be
approached by footpath. Earthworks largely intact. Hadleigh
station (033422).

USES: Hadleigh station is a council depot, Capel under road widening.
SETTING: Low plateau intersected by shallow valleys. Woods and orchards near Hadleigh.

SNAPE JUNCTION–SNAPE   1 mile
East Suffolk Railway
ACT: 1854, 17–18 Vic. Ch xxvi.
OPENED: 1 June 1859 (*gds*).
Incorporated into GER; 7 August 1862.
CLOSED: 7 March 1960 (*gds*).
REMAINS: Bridge north-west of Maltings lightly built across creek. Station house at Snape (391575).
USES: Grazing land.
SETTING: A short branch which descends from the low plateau to cross the marshes and tidal creeks to the Snape Maltings, themselves internationally known for their connections with Benjamin Britten's concerts and the Aldeburgh Festival.

LEISTON–ALDEBURGH   4 miles
East Suffolk Railway
ACT: 1854, 17–18 Vic. Ch xxvi.
OPENED: 1 June 1859.
Incorporated in GER: 7 August 1862.
CLOSED: Sizewell–Aldeburgh: 30 November 1959 (*gds*); Saxmundham–Aldeburgh: 12 September 1966 (*pass*).
REMAINS: Crossing keeper's cottage and platform at Thorpeness (462604), marvellous floral display in summer. Aldeburgh station (459571) partly demolished. Trackbed and minor earthworks can be traced most of the way.
USES: Thorpeness cottage now a private residence.
SETTING: Heath and marshland typical of this part of the Suffolk coast. Aldeburgh is very picturesque, with many literary and musical associations, while Thorpeness is a late and architecturally whimsical small resort made famous by James Barrie.

YARMOUTH–GORLESTON–LOWESTOFT   12¾ miles
Norfolk & Suffolk Joint Committee (GER and M&GNJR)
ACT: 5 July 1898.

OPENED: 13 July 1903.
Operated by LNER: 1 October 1936.
Incorporated in British Railways: 1 January 1948.
CLOSED: 3 July 1967 (*gds*—except Lowestoft North, November 1967); 4 May 1970 (*pass*).
REMAINS: Most earthworks and bridges are still intact, but in Yarmouth district are likely to be levelled in the near future. Hopton (528002) and Corton (541972) are also complete.
USES: Hopton station is the workshop of a boatbuilding company. A housing estate is being built across the trackbed south of Gorleston.
SETTING: Runs along the clifftop a few hundred yards from the sea most of the way, holiday camps, bungalow villages and farmland alternate. Approach to Lowestoft through pleasant northern suburbs.

YARMOUTH SOUTH TOWN–HADDISCOE–BECCLES   12½ miles
Halesworth, Beccles & Haddiscoe Railway/Yarmouth & Haddiscoe Railway amalgamated to form East Suffolk Railway
ACTS: Beccles–Haddiscoe: 5 June 1851.
Haddiscoe–Yarmouth: 7 July 1856.
OPENED: Beccles–Haddiscoe: 20 November 1854 (*gds*); 4 December 1854 (*pass*).
Haddiscoe–Yarmouth: 1 June 1859.
Incorporated in GER: 7 August 1862.
CLOSED: 2 November 1959 (through *pass* and *gds*). Haddiscoe Aldeby: February 1965 (*gds*).
REMAINS: Yarmouth South Town station (519073) has an intact façade with 1950s BR lettering. Haddiscoe (High Level) (459985) is an inter-war concrete-and-brick station with signalbox and parts of the bridges to the north of the Norwich–Lowestoft line. Belton & Burgh station (478027) complete, as is Aldeby station (446945). Earthworks still mostly there, so following the line is relatively easy.
USES: Sunken road uses cutting at Belton. Yarmouth South Town now oil-rig supply office and depot.
SETTING: Long stretches alongside or across the wide alluvial valleys of North-East Suffolk, the Isle of Lothingland and intervening low arable country. A good introduction to the Broads.

YARMOUTH BEACH–GORLESTON $3\frac{1}{4}$ miles
Midland & Great Northern Joint Railway (Lowestoft Junction Railway)
ACT: 1898, 61–2 Vic. Ch cxx.
OPENED: 13 July 1903.
　Operated by LNER: 1 October 1936.
　Incorporated into British Railways: 1 January 1948.
CLOSED: 21 September 1953.
REMAINS: Steel bridge across River Bure (521085). Earthworks at Cobholm Island, south of the Yare. (To be removed shortly.)
SETTING: Breydon Water is a broad expanse of tidal water formerly crossed by the viaduct which dominated the approaches to Yarmouth from the west.

WICKHAM MARKET–FRAMLINGHAM $6\frac{1}{2}$ miles
East Suffolk Railway
ACT: 1854, 17–18 Vic. Ch xxvi.
OPENED: 1 June 1859.
　Incorporated into GER 7 August 1862.
CLOSED: 3 November 1952 (*pass*—except occasional excursions). 19 April 1965 (*gds*).
REMAINS: Most earthworks and bridges are intact as are crossing-keepers' cottages and intermediate stations. Framlingham (285630) much altered but parts still recognisable. Marlesford (326576) & Parham (308607) are intact, the former with a GER coach body on the platform.
USES: Farm services depot at Framlingham. Crossing keepers' cottages and stations at Parham & Marlesford now private houses.
SETTING: The road is within yards of the trackbed at most points along a delightful valley. Framlingham is a very pleasant little town, full of interest and has a castle.

CHAPTER 6: MID-SUFFOLK

THETFORD–BURY ST EDMUNDS $12\frac{3}{4}$ miles
Bury St Edmunds & Thetford Railway
ACT: 5 July 1865.
OPENED: 1 March 1876.
　Incorporated in GER: 1878.

CLOSED: 8 June 1953 (*pass*); 27 June 1960 (*gds*).
REMAINS: Black flint stations at Barnham (862793) and Ingham (857709) where there is also a good overbridge. Light earthworks mostly intact.
USES: Thetford by-pass uses first mile of route to Thetford Bridge. Barnham station now offices for a scrapyard. Ingham is a contractor's company yard and offices.
SETTING: Heath and plantations of the Breckland.

BURY ST EDMUNDS–LONG MELFORD   16½ miles
Great Eastern Railway (originally Eastern Counties Railway)
ACT: 1861 (re-enacted 7 August 1862 under GER Act).
OPENED: 9 August 1865.
CLOSED: 10 April 1961 (*pass*); 19 April 1965 (*gds*).
REMAINS: Heavy earthworks and many bridges throughout. Good bridge in local brick at 895592. Welnetham (897591) intact. Cockfield with a glass-fronted station and cast-iron urinal (904545) is worth a visit. Lavenham (916497) retains station house, platelayers' concrete hut and overbridge (916497).
USES: Refuse pulveriser at Welnetham. Coalyard at Cockfield. Factory in Lavenham station yard. Bury St Edmunds end used as route of new by-pass.
SETTING: The line crosses two watersheds, leaving Bury up the Lark valley, down the Brett valley to Lavenham and then over the next watershed to the Stour at Long Melford. Parkland and orchards are common en route as well as the outstanding medieval town of Lavenham and the medieval-Georgian Long Melford.

HAUGHLEY–LAXFIELD–CRATFIELD AND KENTON–DEBENHAM   27 miles
Mid-Suffolk Light Railway
ACT: Light Railway Order, 1901.
OPENED: Haughley–Laxfield: 20 September 1904 (*gds*); Laxfield–Cratfield: 1906 (*gds*).
Kenton–Debenham (unofficial): 1904.
Incorporated in LNER: 1924.
CLOSED: Kenton–Debenham: 1904 (*gds*); Laxfield Mill–Cratfield: February 1912 (*gds*).
Haughley–Laxfield: 28 July 1952 (*all*).
REMAINS: Abutments at Haughley Junction (042623); abutments of bridge over B1077 on Kenton–Debenham line at 174647, note very mature trees on the embankments either side.

Shallow cutting beside A140 at 120658. Corrugated-iron station building at Horham (215722), platform at Wilby (252732) and cattle pen, wooden station building and part of platform at Laxfield (287725).

USES: Linear scrapyard (120658), modern maltings (102655). Farmyard at Kenton Junction (188669). Part of Laxfield station now used as sports pavilion in the village. Several stretches are used as farm tracks and minor roads, the rest is ploughed-up.

SETTING: Deepest rural Suffolk near the setting for 'Akenfield'. Decayed market towns and villages with some modern farms and a few new factories.

CHAPTER 7: CAMBRIDGE AND DISTRICT

CAMBRIDGE–FORDHAM–MILDENHALL   20¾ miles
Great Eastern Railway
ACT: 1883.
OPENED: Cambridge to Fordham: 2 June 1884. Fordham to Mildenhall: 1 April 1885.
CLOSED: 18 June 1962 (*pass*). 13 July 1964 (*gds*—except Fordham–Burwell). Fordham–Burwell: 19 April 1965 (*gds*).
REMAINS: Light earthworks at intervals of ploughed-over trackbed. Many bridges remain over lifted line throughout. Fordham (618698) Mildenhall (70974) and Barnwell (473597) are easily accessible stations retaining main features of the line.
USES: Sidings at Barnwell. Bridges used as farm tracks across fen waterways. Mildenhall station is a private house.
SETTING: Ran between Fen edge and chalk uplands serving a string of delightful villages and small towns.

GREAT CHESTERFORD–SIX MILE BOTTOM–NEWMARKET   16¾ miles
Newmarket & Chesterford Railway
ACT: 16 July 1846.
OPENED: 3 January 1848 (*gds*); 4 April 1848 (*pass*).
CLOSED: Six Mile Bottom–Great Chesterford: 9 October 1851. (*all*).
REMAINS: Earthworks most of the way from Six Mile Bottom to Great Chesterford. Old Newmarket station (647628) formerly

a goods depot for many years, somewhat decayed but officially preserved.

USES: Linear woodlands alongside the A11. Six Mile Bottom to Newmarket still in use.

SETTING: Chalk downlands crossed by pre-historic dykes and ditches.

ST IVES–HUNTINGDON   5½ miles
Ely & Huntingdon Railway
ACT: 1846, 8–9 Vic. Ch xlviii.
OPENED: 17 August 1847.
Incorporated into East Anglian Railway 1847; GN&GEJR from 1882.
CLOSED: 11 September 1959.
REMAINS: Parts of bridges between Godmanchester and Huntingdon. Some light earthworks.
SETTING: Orchards and Ouse river valley.

CAMBRIDGE–POTTON   17¾ miles
Bedford & Cambridge Railway
ACT: 1860, 23–4 Vic. Ch clxxxiii.
OPENED: 1 August 1862.
Incorporated into LNWR 1865.
CLOSED: 18 April 1966 (*gds*); 1 January (*pass*).
REMAINS: Earthworks and bridges largely intact. Stations at Potton (219412) with B&C roof brackets, Gamlingay (247518) and Old North Road (326546) largely intact. Latter has signalbox and goods shed.
USES: Radio telescope along trackbed (395545). Stations at Potton, Gamlingay and Old North Road are private dwellings.
SETTING: Broad shallow valley of the Bourn Brook.

CHAPTER 8: ESSEX–SUFFOLK BORDERS

CAMBRIDGE–HAVERHILL–SUDBURY   34¾ miles
Colchester, Stour Valley, Sudbury & Halstead Railway
ACT: 1846. 9–10 Vic. Ch lxxvi.
OPENED: Marks Tey–Sudbury: 2 July 1849.
   Sudbury–Haverhill: 9 August 1865.
   Cambridge–Haverhill: 1 June 1865.
   Incorporated in GER: 7 August 1862.
CLOSED: 31 October 1966 (*gds*); 6 March 1967 (*pass*).
REMAINS: Earthworks largely intact. Crossing keepers' cottages

mostly still intact. Station houses and platforms largely intact, Clare (772452) and Glemsford, which has a goods shed (831465), are good representatives. Stoke station is complete with awnings (743437), see also the red brick overbridges nearby. USES: Most of the stations and crossing keepers' cottages are private dwellings. Bartlow station is now called 'Booking Hall'. Clare has been turned into a country park centre and the platform is surrounded by lawns.

SETTING: From Cambridge to beyond Bartlow the line climbs up to 100 metres on the chalklands following the valley of the River Granta. Beyond Haverhill the line then crosses and recrosses the Stour in a valley of outstanding beauty, with villages and towns of exceptional architectural merit.

HAVERHILL–HALSTEAD–CHAPPEL & WAKES COLNE   19½ miles
Colne Valley & Halstead Railway
ACTS: Chappel–Halstead: 30 June 1856.
Halstead–Haverhill: 13 August 1859.
OPENED: Chappel–Halstead: 16 April 1860.
Halstead–Haverhill: 10 May 1863.
Incorporated in LNER: 1 January 1923.
CLOSED: 1 January 1962 (*pass*). Haverhill–Yeldham: 1 January 1962 (*gds*); Halstead–Yeldham: 28 December 1964 (*gds*); Halstead–Chappell: 19 April 1965 (*gds*).
REMAINS: Most earthworks are intact but most bridges retain only their abutments, often heavily eroded and damaged. Earl's Colne (872291) is in exceptionally good order. Halstead and embankments east of Haverhill. Public footpath along trackbed from Yeldham to Hedingham. Halstead station largely demolished apart from platforms (812305). Goods shed and platform at Yeldham (759379). Major bridge across A604 (679448).
USES: Earl's Colne station used as offices. Farm track uses cutting and embankments east of Haverhill. Public footpath along trackbed from Yeldham to Hedingham.
SETTING: Broad pastoral valley with a busy market town and minor industrial settlements.

WIVENHOE–BRIGHTLINGSEA   5 miles
Wivenhoe & Brightlingsea Railway
ACT: 11 July 1861.
OPENED: 18 April 1866.
Purchased by GER in June 1893.

CLOSED: 15 June 1964.
REMAINS: Low embankments most of the way from Wivenhoe to Brightlingsea.
USES: Defence against marshes being flooded. Brightlingsea station (084166) redeveloped.
SETTING: Alongside a long tidal creek used by coasters for Colchester and small sailing craft.

AUDLEY END–SAFFRON WALDEN–BARTLOW $7\frac{1}{4}$ miles
Saffron Walden Railway
ACTS: Audley End–Saffron Walden: 22 July 1861.
Saffron Walden–Bartlow: 22 June 1863.
OPENED: Audley End–Saffron Walden: 21 November 1865.
Saffron Walden–Bartlow: 26 October 1866.
Purchased by GER: 1 January 1877.
CLOSED: 7 September 1964 (*pass*); 28 December 1964 (*gds*).
REMAINS: Infilled branch platform at Audley End station. Earthworks clear and easy to follow from Audley End to Ashdon. Numerous structures in Saffron Walden town. Bartlow station intact (582450), also Acrow Halt platform in Saffron Walden (555389).
USES: Audley End branch area a car park. Saffron Walden part of a garage. Bartlow is a private house. Works and pipe-line agency at Acrow Halt.
SETTING: Steep climb from Cam valley up through very picturesque town of Saffron Walden and across the watershed to upper valley of the Bourn. Land is forested or arable.

CHAPTER 9: NORFOLK–SUFFOLK BORDERS

MELLIS–EYE 3 miles
Mellis & Eye Railway
ACT: 5 July 1865.
OPENED: 2 April 1867.
Incorporated in GER: 1898.
CLOSED: 2 February 1931 (*pass*); 13 July 1964 (*gds*).
REMAINS: Branch platform at Mellis Junction (099745). Bridge under A140 (122741) and several station buildings at Eye (143737).
USES: Agricultural supply complex at Eye station. Most of the trackbed restored to farming.

SETTING: Shallow minor valley deep in rural Suffolk leading to a little-developed market town.

DISS–SCOLE   7 miles
Scole Railway
ACT: None. Private-estate railway.
OPENED: 1850.
CLOSED: 1886.
REMAINS: Abutments near Frenze Hall (135805).

WYMONDHAM–FORNCETT   6¾ miles
Great Eastern Railway
ACT: 1879.
OPENED: 2 May 1881.
CLOSED: 10 September 1939 (*pass*); 4 August 1951 (*gds*).
REMAINS: Turntable pit at Forncett (176945), a reminder of Board of Trade insistence on facilities for turning tender locomotives. Earthworks and bridge abutments throughout. Ashwellthorpe station (161978) intact. Stub south-east from Wymondham.
USES: Ashwellthorpe station is a private house. Stub at Wymondham is used as a storage siding for rolling stock to be scrapped in Norwich.
SETTING: Arable plateau descending into Tas valley.

TIVETSHALL–BECCLES   19½ miles
Waveney Valley Railway
ACTS: Tivetshall–Bungay: 3 July 1851.
    Bungay–Beccles: 4 August 1853.
OPENED: Tivetshall–Harleston: 1 December 1855.
    Harleston–Bungay: 2 November 1860.
    Bungay–Beccles: 2 March 1863.
    Incorporated in GER: 2 March 1863.
CLOSED: 5 January 1953 (*pass*); Harleston–Bungay: 1 February 1960 (*gds*); Bungay–Ditchingham: 3 August 1964 (*gds*); Beccles–Ditchingham: 19 April 1965 (*gds*); Tivetshall–Harleston: 18 April 1966 (*gds*).
REMAINS: Most stations and numerous crossing keepers' cottages intact throughout. Harleston (249839) and Pulham Market (193857) are good examples of mid-nineteenth century stations. Tivetshall branch platform clearly marked (157879). Trackbed easy to follow from Pulham Market to Beccles.

USES: Bungay station yard being redeveloped as an industrial estate (333902). Trackbed immediately west of Harleston station used as an open air store. Homersfield to Earsham used as a road.

SETTING: Tivetshall to Redenhall follows a tributary of the Waveney downhill then the line follows the broad floodplain of the Waveney through a succession of pleasant villages and small towns with several rural parks nearby.

CHAPTER 10: HARBOUR RAILWAYS AND MINOR SPURS

WELLS HARBOUR: 1859–1962. Light earthworks and route easily followed to quayside.

YARMOUTH UNION: 1882–1970. Connection to Yarmouth Beach closed March 1959 but White Swan Yard Coal Depot continued to be served from Vauxhall. Junction visible in roadway.

WISBECH HARBOUR: 1866–1964, M&GNJR. Also GER branch.

KING'S LYNN HARBOUR: 1849. Closed 3 June 1968. Dock branch still open.

KING'S LYNN–SETCHEY: Opened 1920–1921. 2ft 0in gauge, disused by 1954. Sanstone Ltd, no locomotives in later years.

LOWESTOFT KIRKLEY AND SOUTH SIDE: 1859 to 1966 and November 1967 respectively.

LOWESTOFT FISH QUAY: Fish offal from market to departure sidings Lowestoft until 1973.

SUTTON BRIDGE: 1881, failed to develop.

SOUTHWOLD: 1914–1929.

COLCHESTER HYTHE: 1847–1966.

MOUSEHOLD LIGHT RAILWAY: (World War 1)—Norwich Thorpe, via city tramways to factory.

WAGGONWAYS

RIVER LEE NAVIGATION: CHESHUNT (PALMERS RAILWAY) ¾ mile. 1825–? Monorail.

PURFLEET RAILWAY: Two tracks from Thames to chalk quarries. 1½ miles. 3ft 6in gauge. 1805–1907.

Bibliography & Sources

The guide to reading given here is but a part of the vast amount of printed matter available on East Anglian railways and merely indicates where to start on the much more extensive unpublished material. A reasonably complete bibliography which included a century and a half of sources over 10,000 square miles would be far too bulky for this work and only reasonably accessible books, articles and reference sources have been selected. If complete reference to all magazines is required then the Public Record Office, British Transport Collection in Porchester Road London W2, a few yards from Royal Oak station (London Transport—Hammersmith & City line) is the best place to start. County Record Offices are most helpful with local material and the Norfolk and Essex offices are very good in this respect. In addition, many local societies publish bulletins and booklets only available on subscription; leading East Anglian societies include the Cambridge University Railway Club, the Norfolk Railway Society and many others.

Original sources include the Acts of Parliament, the Parliamentary enquiries which were held in disputed cases (these are often very revealing but may run to hundreds and even thousands of closely-printed pages), *Herapath's* and the *Railway News* (which kept Victorian shareholders apprised of the often poor fortunes of their investments) and the minute books of the individual companies. Researching the full history of even a short branch line is a monumental but rewarding task.

The following abbreviations have been used:
The Railway Magazine—RM
Railway World—RW   *Trains Illustrated*—TI

GENERAL

Author	Title	Publication
C. J. ALLEN	The Great Eastern Railway, *5th Edition*	Ian Allan 1968
CHARLES H. GRINLING	The History of the Great Northern Railway	Allen & Unwin 1966
B. BAXTER	Stone Blocks and Iron Rails–Tramroads	David & Charles 1966
H. G. LEWIN	The Railway Mania and Its Aftermath	London 1936
C. J. ALLEN	The London & North Eastern Railway	Ian Allan 1966
J. SIMMONS	The Railways of Britain	London 1961
W. L. STEEL	History of the LNWR	London 1914
R. H. CLARK	A Short History of the M&GNJR	Norwich 1967
A J. WROTTESLEY	The Midland & Great Northern Joint Railway	David & Charles 1970
R. C. RILEY	Great Eastern Album	Ian Allan 1968
E. L. AHRONS	Locomotive and Train Working in the Latter Part of the 19th Century	Heffers, Cambridge 1952
RAILWAY CLEARING HOUSE	Railway Junction Diagrams 1915	David & Charles 1969
	Bradshaw's Railway Manual 1850–1923	
	Bradshaw's Official Guide 1839–1959	
C. R. CLINKER & J. M. FIRTH	Register of Closed Passenger Stations & Goods Depots	Padstow 1970
D. I. GORDON	Regional History of British Railways *Vol V*	David & Charles 1968

NORTH-EAST NORFOLK

H. D. WATTS	Melton Constable	Northern Geographer
A. HANSON	Poppyland and one way to it	RM 1898
G. A. SEKON	Railways in Poppyland	RM 1904
E. TUDDENHAM	M&GN Route to Cromer	RW 1964
E. TUDDENHAM	Norfolk & Suffolk Joint	RW 1966
W. W. BAYLES	Mundesley to Cromer	TI 1953
A. MAXWELL	The M&GNJR (1) Its Traffic	RM 1936
F. T. GILLFORD	The M&GNJR (2) Its Locomotives	RM 1936
V. R. WEBSTER	Train Working at Cromer	RM 1954

MID-ESSEX AND NORTH-EAST HERTFORDSHIRE

P. J. NORRIS	Maldon East to Witham	RM 1960
G. DRUCE	Hertford to Welwyn	RW 1951
B. D. J. WALSH	Maldon to Woodham Ferrers	RM 1957
P. GENTRY	Elsenham & Thaxted	RW 1952
N. J. STAPLETON	Kelvedon & Tollesbury Light Railway	Bledlow Press 1962
B. D. J. WALSH	The Ware, Hadham & Buntingford Railway	RM 1953

NORTH-WEST NORFOLK

G. BODY & R. EASTLEIGH	The East Anglian Railway	Transrail 1967
D. I. GORDON	Dereham to King's Lynn	RM 1958
E. W. POTTER	GE in West Norfolk	RM 1910
B. D. J. WALSH	Thetford & Swaffham	RM 1953
J. F. CAIRNS	Norfolk Lines of the LNER	RM 1929
MAXWELL & GILLFORD	The M&GNJR (see above)	RM 1936
R. S. MCNAUGHT	Farewell to the Leicesters	RM 1959
H. J. SAWARD	Wolferton and Sandringham	GER Magazine 1911

FENS

G. BODY & R. EASTLEIGH	The East Anglian Railway	Transrail 1967
R. GOODYEAR	The Wisbech & Upwell Tramway	RM 1957
GADSDEN, WHETMATH & STAFFORD	Wisbech & Upwell Tramway	Branch Line Handbooks 1967
ARTHUR RANDELL	Fenland Railwaymen	RKP 1968
J. F. CAIRNS	Fruit Traffic on the GER	RM 1923

EAST SUFFOLK

L. A. SMITH	Aldeburgh–Saxmundham	TI 1957
S. DUNANT	Southwold	RM 1899
C. LEE	Southwold	RM 1929
A. TAYLOR & E. TONKS	The Southwold Railway	Ian Allan 1950/65
E. TUDDENHAM	The Norfolk & Suffolk Joint	RW 1966
D. BARRIE & B. D. J. WALSH	Railways of East Suffolk	RM 1954

MID-SUFFOLK

N. A. COMFORT	The Mid-Suffolk Light Railway	Oakwood Press 1963
R. E. VINCENT	The Mid-Suffolk Light Railway	TI 1952
B. D. J. WALSH	Railways to Thetford	RM 1953

CAMBRIDGE & DISTRICT

J. T. LAWRENCE	Cambridge to Bletchley	RM 1910
V. R. WEBSTER	To Cambridge by Midland	TI 1957
G. F. OAKMAN	Railways at Cambridge	RM 1954
R. B. FELLOWS	The Newmarket & Chesterford Railway	RM 1930

ESSEX–SUFFOLK BORDERS

C. LANGLEY ALDRICH	The Brightlingsea Branch LNER	RM 1947
J. F. GAIRNS	The Colne Valley Railway	RM 1923
B. D. J. WALSH	The Stour Valley Railway	RM 1951

NORFOLK–SUFFOLK BORDERS

G. BODY	Eye–Mellis Branch	RM 1959
B. D. J. WALSH	The Waveney Valley Railway	RM 1957
N. A. BRUNDELL & K. J. WHITTAKER	The Scole Railway	RM 1957

Acknowledgements

No book of this kind could be written without building up a great debt to others. Professor Patmore of Hull University has read, criticised and suggested amendments to the manuscript, being an invaluable source of information on style, syntax and presentation. Chats with many members of the Norfolk Railway Society, the M&GN, and North Norfolk Railway Societies have given me leads, memories and access to old material which has been incorporated here.

My family has accompanied me on many of the safaris to lost railways and they developed eagle eyes for detail spotting. During the research and write-up period, my wife has plied me with coffee and all home comforts, so invaluable to a writer.

The libraries used have been helpful beyond the immediate calls of duty; to the Norfolk County libraries used, especially the Colman & Rye library in Norwich, to the University libraries of East Anglia, London, Leicester and Cambridge, a special thank-you. The Public Record Offices at Portchester Road, Chancery Lane and the Census Records Department have all been great reservoirs of useful information, with a helpful staff.

Finally, I am grateful to those photographers who have allowed me to use the photographs which appear in the book.

Index